Beyond Words: Navigating the Secrets of Human Mind and Behavior

By

Chase Hunter

OMA International Publications

Table of Contents

INTRODUCTION

In the dimly lit interrogation room, a seasoned detective leans forward, eyes locked on the suspect. The air is thick with tension, each moment heavy with the weight of unspoken truths. Across the table, a slight twitch at the corner of the mouth, a barely noticeable shift in posture, and the detective knows - they've just uncovered the lie that will crack the case wide open. This pivotal moment, where keen observation meets intuitive insight, underscores a profound truth: the ability to read people can alter the course of events, unlock deeper connections, and unveil the hidden tapestry of human behavior.

My journey into the labyrinth of human interactions began early in my career, driven by a relentless curiosity about what lies beneath the surface of our exchanges. With years of experience marrying the precision of professional investigative techniques with the nuanced understanding of intuitive insights, I've dedicated myself to unraveling the complexities of human behavior. My passion is not just in the pursuit of this knowledge but in sharing these discoveries, empowering you to navigate the intricate world of human interactions with confidence and empathy.

"Beyond Words: Navigating the Secrets of Human Mind and Behavior" is born of this vision. It represents a bridge between the analytical rigor of body and mind reading and the instinctual realm of gut feelings and intuition. This book is crafted for you - detectives, professionals, young adults, and every inquisitive soul in between, offering a key to unlock the mysteries of human behavior, detect deception, and forge authentic connections that transcend words.

As we embark on this journey together, you'll be introduced to the foundational pillars of body language, micro expressions, and beyond, venturing into the digital realm and across cultural landscapes. Through real-life case studies, practical exercises, and thoughtful ethical discussions, this book provides a holistic toolkit for mastering the art of reading people.

What sets this book apart is its unique alchemy of scientific rigor and everyday wisdom, offering insights that are as applicable in the boardroom as they are at the dinner table. Grounded in the latest psychological research and enriched with cultural empathy, this guide is your compass in the quest for deeper human connections.

As we turn the page to this transformative journey, I invite you to embrace the lessons within these pages. Let them be your guide to navigating the secrets of the human mind and behavior, enhancing your awareness, and enriching your interactions with others.

To echo the sentiments of esteemed colleagues and readers who have journeyed with me thus far, "This book opens eyes, minds, and hearts to the unspoken language that shapes our world." Together, let's unlock the power of beyond words, stepping into a realm of understanding, confidence, and connection that will redefine the way you see yourself and others.

Welcome to "Beyond Words." Your journey to mastering the art of reading people begins now.

CHAPTER 1

The Language of the Body Unveiled

Within moments of meeting someone, a complex web of judgments, assumptions, and predictions unfurls in our minds, often without our conscious awareness. These initial assessments, made with lightning speed, lay the groundwork for future interactions, for better or worse. This chapter delves into the intricacies of first impressions, shedding light on their formation, influence, and the underlying biological and psychological mechanisms at play. Through understanding these processes, we gain the ability to navigate social landscapes more adeptly, ensuring the impressions we leave behind are as intentional as they are impactful.

1.1 The Science of First Impressions: Decoding Instant Judgements

When we meet someone for the first time, our brains operate on overdrive, piecing together a myriad of visual and auditory cues to form an immediate judgment. This process, rapid and largely subliminal, shapes our perceptions and interactions in profound ways.

Instant Analysis

Research reveals that first impressions are formed within milliseconds of encountering someone. A study published in "Psychological Science" suggests that even a glance lasting a fraction of a second can influence our judgments of a person's attractiveness, likeability, trustworthiness, competence, and aggressiveness. These snap judgments stem from our brain's instinctual drive to quickly categorize and assess new stimuli, a mechanism critical for decision-making and social navigation.

Visual Dominance

The visual aspect of our initial encounters holds significant weight in the formation of first impressions. Before a word is exchanged, our brains analyze facial features, body language, posture, and attire, using these visual cues as the basis for our judgments. This reliance on visual information can be attributed to the brain's predilection for processing complex visual stimuli efficiently, a trait that has evolved over millennia. The power of visual cues is such that they can override subsequent verbal information, highlighting the importance of non-verbal communication in first encounters.

Evolutionary Perspectives

The roots of our reliance on non-verbal cues and the swift formation of first impressions can be traced back to our evolutionary history. In the ancestral environment, the ability to quickly evaluate whether an individual was a friend or foe, trustworthy or deceitful, was crucial for survival. This evolutionary backdrop underscores the importance of non-verbal communication as a survival tool, enabling our ancestors to navigate social hierarchies and form alliances. The remnants of this evolutionary past persist today, influencing our social interactions and decision-making processes.

Modifying Impressions

While the initial impressions we form are powerful, they are not set in stone. Through strategic self-presentation and behavior modification, it is possible to influence and alter the first impressions we make. Consider the scenario of a job interview, where stakes are high, and the desire to project competence and confidence is paramount. Here, small adjustments in posture, making deliberate eye contact, and dressing appropriately can significantly impact the interviewer's perception. Similarly, being mindful of our body language during social encounters can help us project the qualities we wish to be associated with, such as openness, friendliness, or reliability.

By understanding the mechanisms underlying first impressions, we empower ourselves to navigate social interactions more effectively. This knowledge enables us to present ourselves in a manner that aligns with our intentions, fostering positive perceptions that pave the way for fruitful relationships and opportunities.

1.2 Unlocking the Power of Microexpressions: A Window to True Emotions

Microexpressions serve as fleeting windows into an individual's genuine emotions, often bypassing their conscious attempts to mask feelings. These rapid, involuntary facial expressions occur in as little as 1/25th of a second, revealing emotions such as joy, surprise, anger, fear, disgust, contempt, or sadness. Despite their brevity, microexpressions are universal across cultures, pointing to a shared human emotional experience.

To tap into the subtle world of microexpressions and interpret them accurately, a focused and educated eye is crucial. Start by enhancing your observational skills in everyday interactions. Pay close attention to the faces of those around you, noting any quick flashes of emotion that might contradict their spoken words. Tools such as videos of facial expressions slowed down can aid in this training, allowing you to familiarize yourself with the nuances of each emotion.

Recognizing microexpressions can significantly elevate one's emotional intelligence (EI), enhancing the ability to empathize and connect with others. EI involves understanding one's own emotions as well as those of others, a skill that is deeply enriched by the ability to detect these brief emotional signals. It is this deeper understanding that enables more meaningful interactions, as recognizing genuine feelings can guide how we respond to and engage with others.

In professional settings, the ability to read microexpressions can be particularly transformative. For instance, in negotiations, detecting a fleeting expression of dissatisfaction or doubt on an opponent's face can provide invaluable insight into their true feelings about the deal, allowing for adjustments in strategy. In leadership roles, recognizing signs of unrest or dissatisfaction early on can help address issues before they escalate, fostering a healthier work environment.

In personal relationships, this skill fosters deeper connections and trust. Being responsive to a partner's unspoken feelings, perhaps noticing a brief flash of sadness that prompts a conversation, can strengthen the bond between individuals. It demonstrates attentiveness and care, showing that one is truly seen and understood beyond words.

However, it's essential to approach the interpretation of microexpressions with sensitivity and discretion. While they can offer glimpses into genuine feelings, they are pieces of a larger emotional puzzle. It's crucial to consider the context and other verbal and non-verbal cues to form a more accurate understanding of an individual's emotional state.

1.3 The Art of Mirroring: Building Rapport Without Words

Mirroring, a subtle yet powerful form of non-verbal communication, involves subtly mimicking another person's body language, gestures, and facial expressions. This phenomenon, deeply rooted in our psychological makeup, plays a pivotal role in establishing connection and trust without the need for spoken words. Its effectiveness lies in its ability to create a sense of similarity and empathy, signaling that we are in tune with the person we are interacting with.

Psychological Foundations

The psychological underpinnings of mirroring behavior trace back to the concept of "mirror neurons" discovered in the early 1990s. These neurons fire both when we perform an action and when we observe the same action performed by someone else, essentially allowing us to "mirror" the other's movement in our minds. This mirroring mechanism is thought to be fundamental in understanding others' actions and intentions and fostering empathy. When we mirror someone's body language, we activate these neurons, creating a bridge of understanding and shared experience that naturally leads to increased rapport and trust.

Mirroring in Practice

In practice, mirroring manifests in various scenarios, enhancing communication and connection. For example, during a critical business meeting, if one participant leans forward, and the other subtly mirrors this action, it creates an unspoken agreement of engagement and interest. Similarly, in a therapeutic setting, a counselor might mirror a client's sitting posture or head tilts, fostering a safe space where the client feels understood and validated.

In social settings, mirroring can play a crucial role in forming new relationships. When meeting someone for the first time, consciously adopting a similar stance or mimicking their smile can lead to a more favorable interaction, as it subconsciously communicates likeness and acceptance.

Mirroring does not necessitate a precise duplication of the other person's behavior; instead, it's about capturing the essence of their gestures and posture in a way that feels natural. This can include matching the pace of someone's speech, adopting a similar posture, or using comparable hand gestures during a conversation.

Boundaries and Ethics

While mirroring is a potent tool in enhancing interpersonal connections, it's vital to approach its use with a keen sense of ethics and respect for personal boundaries. Overuse or exaggerated mirroring might come across as mimicry, potentially making the other person feel uncomfortable or even mocked. The key is subtlety and maintaining a genuine intention behind the action - the goal is to foster connection, not to manipulate.

Practicing ethical mirroring means being mindful of the context and the other person's openness to engagement. It's crucial to read the situation accurately and gauge whether your attempts at mirroring are being well-received. If the individual seems to withdraw or appears uncomfortable, it's important to respect their cues and adjust your approach accordingly.

Self-awareness

Effective mirroring starts with self-awareness, both of our own body language and that of others. Cultivating an awareness of how we present ourselves and how others perceive us can provide insights into how best to mirror in a given situation. This involves paying close attention to the subtleties of interactions, noting not just what is being mirrored but also the timing and context.

A practical way to enhance self-awareness is through observation and reflection. Take moments in your day to observe how others interact and how their body language syncs or diverges. Reflect on your interactions, considering how your body language may have influenced the outcome. This practice can not only improve your mirroring skills but also deepen your understanding of non-verbal communication as a whole.

For those keen on developing this skill, here are a few exercises:

- **Observation Exercise**: Spend time in a public place, like a café, and discreetly observe interactions between people. Notice how individuals mirror each other's body language and consider how it affects their communication.

- **Journaling Prompt**: After a significant interaction, jot down notes about the body language you observed and mirrored. Reflect on how mirroring affected the interaction's outcome.

- **Practice with a Partner**: Engage in a conversation with a friend or family member where you consciously mirror their body language. Afterwards, discuss the experience and how it felt from both perspectives.

Incorporating these strategies can significantly refine one's ability to use mirroring effectively, enhancing connections in every walk of life, from professional endeavors to personal relationships. By approaching mirroring with mindfulness, respect, and a genuine desire to connect, we can navigate social landscapes with greater empathy and understanding.

1.4 Posture and Power: How Our Bodies Shape Our Minds

The silent language of our bodies speaks volumes before we even utter a word. The way we carry ourselves not only influences the perceptions of those around us but also deeply impacts our internal state, molding our feelings of confidence and self-assurance. This intricate dance between posture and perception forms the bedrock of our social interactions and personal well-being.

Posture and Perception

The alignment and positioning of our body are potent indicators of our mental state, intentions, and self-esteem. A slouched posture, with shoulders hunched forward and head down, often signals withdrawal, low confidence, or defensiveness. Conversely, standing tall with shoulders back and head held high conveys confidence, openness, and readiness to engage. This non-verbal communication is a two-way street, affecting not just how others perceive us but also how we perceive ourselves. The feedback from our posture feeds into our mental state, reinforcing feelings of strength or vulnerability.

Power Poses

The concept of "power poses," popularized by social psychologist Amy Cuddy, brings to light the profound impact of expansive, open postures on our psychological state. Adopting these poses, even for a few minutes, can lead to measurable changes in hormone levels, increasing testosterone (associated with dominance and confidence) and decreasing cortisol (associated with stress). This physiological shift can enhance feelings of power and readiness to face challenges, demonstrating the profound interconnection between body and mind.

The Feedback Loop

The relationship between posture and mental state is deeply cyclical, creating a feedback loop that can either uplift or undermine us. When we adopt a posture that signals power and confidence, our brain receives a message that we are in control, capable, and unthreatened, which in turn, encourages us to maintain that physical stance. Conversely, a defensive or closed posture sends signals of vulnerability or unease to the brain, potentially leading to a downward spiral of decreased confidence. Recognizing and intentionally influencing this feedback loop can be a powerful tool for personal empowerment.

Implementing Changes

Incorporating more powerful, confident postures into daily life is a practical step toward enhancing well-being and efficacy in social interactions. Here are strategies to foster positive changes:

- **Mindful Observation**: Begin by observing your default posture during various daily activities. Noticing tendencies toward slouching or closing off can be the first step towards change.

- **Adjustment Reminders**: Set regular reminders on your phone or computer to check and adjust your posture. Over time, these conscious adjustments can evolve into a habit of maintaining a more open, confident stance.

- **Power Pose Practice**: Allocate a few minutes each day to practice power poses. This could be in the privacy of your home or office. Consider doing this before challenging situations, such as interviews or important meetings, to harness the psychological benefits.

- **Ergonomic Evaluation**: Consider the ergonomics of your workspace. Chairs, desks, and computer setups that encourage poor posture can be detrimental to your physical and psychological well-being. Making adjustments to support a healthier posture can have lasting benefits.

- **Physical Activity**: Engage in activities that strengthen the core and improve posture, such as yoga, Pilates, or strength training. A strong core supports a more upright, confident posture naturally.

- **Reflective Practice**: At the end of each day, reflect on moments when you felt confident and in control. Correlate these feelings with your posture at the time, reinforcing the connection between how you carry yourself and how you feel.

The intricate relationship between posture and power underscores the importance of body awareness in shaping our mental state and influencing how we are perceived by others. By adopting strategies that encourage more powerful, confident postures, we can open the door to enhanced self-esteem, reduced stress, and more positive social interactions. This conscious manipulation of our non-verbal signals allows us to not only communicate strength to others but to reinforce it within ourselves, laying the foundation for a more empowered and confident presence in the world.

1.5 The Eyes Have It: The Secrets Hidden in Gaze and Blink Rate

The Windows to the Soul

The power of the eyes in communication cannot be overstated. Through eye behavior—where we look, how long we maintain eye contact, and even how frequently we blink—we communicate volumes about our internal state, intentions, and feelings towards the person we are interacting with. Eye contact, in particular, plays a pivotal role. Maintaining it can signify interest, confidence, and sincerity, while avoiding eye contact might suggest discomfort, disinterest, or even deceit. However, it's the subtleties within these behaviors that often provide the most profound insights. For instance, a glance held a moment too long might reveal hidden affections, or a sudden shift away might indicate discomfort or disagreement with what's being discussed.

Cultural Variations

The interpretation of eye behavior is far from universal, deeply influenced by cultural norms and values. In some cultures, direct eye contact is seen as a sign of respect and attentiveness, a way to demonstrate you are fully engaged and valuing the interaction. In contrast, in other cultures, particularly some Asian cultures, prolonged eye contact might be perceived as confrontational or disrespectful, especially if it's between individuals of different social hierarchies. This cultural diversity in understanding eye behavior underscores the importance of being culturally sensitive and aware, especially in our increasingly globalized world. Recognizing and adapting to the cultural nuances of eye behavior can prevent misunderstandings and foster smoother interactions across cultural divides.

Blink Rate and Stress

Another fascinating aspect of eye behavior is the correlation between blink rate and stress levels. Under normal conditions, the average person blinks about 15-20 times per minute. However, this rate can increase significantly under stress or cognitive load. In high-stakes situations, such as interrogations or intense negotiations, a noticeable increase in someone's blink rate can signal that they're under stress or possibly being deceptive. However, it's crucial to consider this within a broader context, as numerous factors can influence blink rate, including environmental irritants or certain medical conditions. Despite these variables, when combined with other non-verbal cues and within a clear context, blink rate can serve as a valuable indicator of psychological stress.

Enhancing Connection

Eye behavior holds tremendous potential to deepen connections in conversations. Here are some strategies to consider:

- **Mindful Eye Contact**: Striking the right balance in eye contact is key. Aim for a level that feels engaged but not overwhelming. A good rule of thumb is the 50/70 rule, maintaining eye contact 50% of the time while speaking and 70% while listening, to communicate interest and confidence.

- **Noticing the 'Eye Smile'**: Often, genuine emotions can be spotted in the crinkling at the corners of the eyes, sometimes referred to as "Duchenne markers." This subtle cue can indicate genuine happiness or amusement and is a sign of a true, heartfelt connection.

- **The Power of the Pupil**: Pupil dilation is another involuntary response that can signal emotional or intellectual engagement. While it's more challenging to observe, in well-lit environments, noticing someone's pupils dilating during a conversation can indicate that they find the topic or the person engaging.

- **Synchronized Blinking**: Interestingly, people who are in sync during a conversation may start to blink at the same time. Paying attention to this can be a subtle indicator of how well two people are connecting.

- **Practicing Active Listening**: Using eye behavior to signal active listening involves nodding, maintaining appropriate eye contact, and using facial expressions that mirror the speaker's emotions. This creates a feedback loop that enhances the speaker's sense of being heard and understood.

In implementing these strategies, it's vital to remain authentic. Eye behavior should feel natural, not forced, as authenticity in non-verbal communication fosters genuine connections. Moreover, being observant of the other person's comfort level with eye contact and adjusting accordingly can make the interaction more comfortable and meaningful for both parties.

The nuances of eye behavior offer a window into the thoughts and emotions of those around us, providing insights that transcend words. By becoming more attuned to these subtle cues and respecting the cultural contexts in which they occur, we can navigate social interactions with greater empathy and understanding. Whether it's through the confidence conveyed in direct eye contact, the stress revealed in an increased blink rate, or the connection felt through synchronized blinking, the eyes indeed have it—serving as powerful tools in the art of reading people.

1.6 The Hidden Language of Feet and Legs: Unspoken Truths

While the face and hands often command our attention in the realm of body language, the feet and legs offer a rich tapestry of cues that are equally telling. Grounded and less consciously controlled, the way we position and move our lower limbs can provide clear insights into our genuine emotions and intentions. This segment explores the subtle, yet profound, language of feet and legs, shedding light on how these often-overlooked aspects of body language can unveil truths hidden in plain sight.

Directional Cues

The direction in which our feet point can serve as a reliable indicator of our true intentions and interests. In social or professional gatherings, a person's feet might be aimed towards an individual they find most intriguing or attractive, even if their gaze and conversation involve someone else. This cue, rooted in our instinctive approach behavior, reveals where our genuine interest lies, bypassing the more controlled social façade we might present. Similarly, in situations where someone desires to exit a conversation or environment, their feet might subtly point towards the nearest exit, signaling an unconscious readiness to leave.

Comfort and Discomfort

Shifts in leg posture can also signal changes in a person's comfort level, offering clues to their emotional state that might not be apparent from their facial expressions or verbal communication. For instance, a relaxed stance with weight evenly distributed or a gentle crossing of the legs can indicate a state of ease and openness. On the flip side, tightly crossed legs or a locked knee position might suggest discomfort or defensiveness. These shifts can occur subtly during an interaction, providing real-time feedback on how well the conversation is being received and whether the other person feels comfortable and engaged.

Crossed Legs

The act of crossing one's legs, while seemingly simple, can convey a range of meanings based on the context and accompanying body language. In a professional setting, crossed legs might be perceived as a closed-off posture, especially if combined with crossed arms, suggesting that the person is mentally, emotionally, or even physically withdrawing from the interaction. Contrastingly, a more casual cross of the legs, particularly when accompanied by open and engaged upper body language, might merely indicate a comfortable resting position rather than a defensive stance. Deciphering the meaning behind crossed legs requires careful consideration of the broader context, including the environment, the nature of the interaction, and other non-verbal cues being presented.

Detecting Deception

Feet and leg movements can also be instrumental in detecting deception. When someone is being untruthful, their body often exhibits stress responses that can manifest in their lower limbs. For instance, a sudden increase in foot movement, such as tapping or shuffling, might indicate nervousness or the psychological discomfort associated with lying. Similarly, when someone takes a stance that appears too rigid or still, it might be a conscious attempt to control their body language, a common behavior when someone is trying to conceal the truth. These indicators, while subtle, can provide valuable insights when assessing the veracity of someone's words.

In understanding the language of feet and legs, it becomes clear that our lower limbs play a critical role in non-verbal communication. By tuning into these subtle cues, we can gain deeper insights into the emotions and intentions of those around us, enriching our interactions and allowing us to navigate social landscapes with greater awareness and sensitivity. Whether it's recognizing the directional cues that reveal someone's true interest, interpreting changes in leg posture as signs of comfort or discomfort, understanding the context-dependent meaning of crossed legs, or detecting the subtle signs of deception, the language of feet and legs is a vital component of the broader conversation happening beyond words.

1.7 Personal Space: The Invisible Boundaries of Comfort

In the tapestry of human interaction, personal space acts as the unseen barrier that governs our comfort and intimacy with others. This invisible buffer zone, varying in size from one person to another, is where most of our non-verbal communication unfolds. Its invasion, intentional or not, can trigger a cascade of psychological responses, from discomfort to outright distress, significantly impacting the dynamics of an encounter.

Defining Personal Space

Personal space is essentially the physical distance we maintain between ourselves and others. It's a protective bubble that helps us feel secure and in control of our environment. Psychologists highlight its role in safeguarding our autonomy and managing sensory input from the outside world. When this space is respected, we tend to feel calm and collected; when breached, it can lead to anxiety or aggression, a primal response rooted in our instinct for self-preservation.

Cultural Differences

The dimensions of personal space are not universally fixed but fluctuate widely across cultures. In some societies, close physical proximity and touch are commonplace and signify warmth and friendliness. In contrast, others prize a greater separation, viewing it as a sign of respect and personal dignity. For instance, in crowded countries like Japan, the concept of personal space is adapted to the reality of daily life, leading to a higher tolerance for proximity in public settings. However, this does not negate the individual's need for a personal bubble; it merely adjusts its scale. Understanding these cultural nuances is crucial in today's globalized world to avoid misinterpretations and foster harmonious cross-cultural interactions.

Invasion of Space

When someone steps uninvited into our personal space, it can be perceived as a threat or a sign of dominance, eliciting a fight or flight response. The nature of this invasion and our reaction to it can be influenced by several factors, including our relationship with the invader, the setting, and our current emotional state. For example, a close friend leaning in during a conversation might be welcomed, whereas a stranger doing the same in a queue might trigger discomfort. This response is also mediated by our personal experiences and boundaries, making some individuals more sensitive to space intrusions than others.

Navigating Spaces

In navigating the complex dance of human interaction without encroaching on personal boundaries, consider the following strategies:

- **Observe and Adapt**: Pay close attention to body language and verbal cues that indicate how comfortable someone is with the distance between you. If you notice signs of discomfort, such as stepping back, crossing arms, or minimal eye contact, it's wise to adjust your position accordingly.

- **Ask if Unsure**: In situations where the appropriate distance isn't clear, it's respectful to ask for the other person's preference. This simple act of consideration can go a long way in building trust and rapport.

- **Consider the Context**: Be mindful of the context of your interaction. A crowded bus might necessitate closer proximity than a spacious office, and adapting to these situational demands shows social awareness and sensitivity.

- **Respect Cultural Norms**: When interacting with individuals from different cultural backgrounds, research and respect their norms regarding personal space. This not only prevents discomfort but also conveys respect for their cultural practices.

- **Personal Space in Professional Settings**: In professional environments, maintaining a slightly larger distance can signal respect and professionalism. Observing how colleagues and superiors navigate space can provide valuable cues on the normative distances within that specific setting.

- **Adjusting to Digital Spaces**: In the realm of digital communication, respecting personal space translates into respecting boundaries around time and availability. Avoiding late-night messages or excessive contact can mirror the respect we show for physical personal space in face-to-face interactions.

In recognizing and honoring the invisible boundaries of personal space, we facilitate smoother, more respectful interactions. This sensitivity to the unspoken rules governing our engagements can enrich our social experiences, allowing for deeper connections built on mutual respect and understanding. By being attuned to the nuances of personal space, both in our culture and in those we encounter, we navigate social landscapes with grace, fostering positive relations in a diverse world.

1.8 The Hands Tell All: From Gestures to Hidden Messages

In the rich tapestry of non-verbal communication, hands play a starring role, capable of expressing a vast array of sentiments, from the most subtle of welcomes to the fiercest displays of defiance. This segment shines a light on the multifaceted language of hand gestures, exploring their potential to convey complex messages, signal cultural affiliations, and even betray unspoken truths.

Gestural Communication

The spectrum of messages that can be communicated through hand gestures is astonishingly broad. A thumbs-up can signal approval or agreement, a clenched fist might express solidarity or resistance, and a simple wave serves as a universal greeting. Each gesture, depending on its execution and context, carries distinct meanings. In professional settings, the way we use our hands can significantly impact the reception of our message. Presenters, for instance, who employ open-handed gestures at chest level, are often perceived as more engaging and trustworthy compared to those who keep their hands hidden or engage in fidgety movements.

Cultural Sensitivity

The interpretation of hand gestures can vary dramatically across different cultures, making cultural sensitivity a crucial aspect of effectively employing this form of communication. For example, the OK sign, formed by connecting the thumb and forefinger into a circle, conveys positive affirmation in many Western cultures. However, in Brazil, the same gesture is considered offensive. Similarly, the thumbs-up sign is interpreted as a rude gesture in parts of the Middle East. Thus, understanding the cultural context is paramount to avoid miscommunication and ensure that the intended message is accurately conveyed.

The Truth in Palms

The positioning of the palms during interaction can profoundly influence perceptions of openness and honesty. Open palms have been associated with truthfulness and sincerity, inviting trust and fostering a sense of security in conversations. In contrast, closed palms, or hands hidden from view, can trigger suspicion, as they are often perceived as signals of withholding information or deceit. This perception is deeply ingrained, with open hand gestures historically seen as a sign of unarmed peace. In negotiations or discussions, consciously employing open palm gestures can thus subtly sway the dynamic in favor of mutual understanding and agreement.

Hands as Deception Indicators

While the face might be the primary focus in attempts to mask deceit, the hands often reveal what one is truly feeling or thinking. Certain hand movements can serve as red flags for dishonesty, providing clues for the keen observer. For instance, excessive fidgeting, such as tapping fingers, playing with jewelry, or repeatedly adjusting one's tie, might indicate nervousness or discomfort associated with deception. Covering the mouth or touching the nose during conversation, actions often performed subconsciously, can also suggest that the speaker is not being entirely truthful. These cues, however, should be interpreted with caution and in conjunction with other non-verbal and verbal signals to form a more accurate assessment of credibility.

In delving into the silent discourse of hand gestures, it becomes evident that our hands are powerful tools in conveying emotions, intentions, and even hidden truths. By harnessing the expressive potential of our hands with awareness and sensitivity, we can navigate the nuances of communication more effectively, bridging gaps and building stronger connections with those around us.

CHAPTER 2

Emotional Intelligence: The Key to Deeper Human Connections

In our daily lives, moments big and small are shaped by the emotions that surge within us and between us. From the joy that bubbles up during a friend's wedding to the frustration of a delayed morning commute, emotions color our world and influence our interactions. Yet, understanding and managing these emotions, both in ourselves and others, is a skill often left unexplored, despite its profound impact on our lives. This chapter delves into the core of emotional intelligence, unraveling its components and offering practical strategies to enhance our capacity for emotional understanding and self-regulation.

Understanding Self-Awareness

Self-awareness is the cornerstone of emotional intelligence. It involves recognizing our own emotions as they happen and understanding the influence they have on our thoughts and actions. Imagine you're in a meeting and suddenly feel irritated by a colleague's comment. Self-awareness allows you to identify this irritation, consider why the comment bothered you, and decide how to respond in a constructive manner. This skill prevents emotions from hijacking our behavior, enabling more thoughtful interactions.

Strategies for Enhancing Self-Awareness:

- **Keep an Emotion Journal**: Spend a few minutes each day writing about the emotions you felt and the events that triggered them. Over time, patterns will emerge, offering insights into your emotional triggers and reactions.

- **Mindfulness Meditation**: Regular practice helps you observe your thoughts and feelings without judgment, increasing your awareness of them in the moment.

- **Ask for Feedback**: Sometimes, others see aspects of our behavior we're blind to. Constructive feedback from friends or colleagues can provide valuable perspectives on how our emotions influence our interactions.

Strategies for Self-Regulation

Once we're aware of our emotions, self-regulation comes into play. This skill involves managing our emotions, especially in stressful situations, to respond in ways that align with our values and goals. It's the difference between snapping at a colleague over a minor mistake and taking a moment to calm down before responding.

Techniques for Practicing Self-Regulation:

- **Pause Before Responding**: When you feel strong emotions, take a deep breath and count to ten. This brief pause can give you the space you need to choose a more thoughtful response.

- **Identify Alternative Responses**: In your emotion journal, for situations that didn't go well, write down other ways you could have responded. This exercise can help you think of more constructive responses in future situations.

- **Practice Relaxation Techniques**: Techniques such as deep breathing, progressive muscle relaxation, or visualizing a calming scene can help reduce the intensity of your emotions, making them easier to manage.

Impact on Reading People

Enhancing our emotional intelligence not only improves how we manage our own emotions but also how we read and respond to the emotions of others. When we're in tune with our feelings, we become more sensitive to the emotional cues of those around us. This sensitivity can transform interactions, allowing us to respond to others with empathy and understanding rather than judgment or indifference.

Consider a friend sharing a personal challenge. If you're self-aware and self-regulated, you're more likely to recognize the emotions your friend is experiencing and respond in a way that shows genuine support and concern, rather than offering a distracted or generic response.

Emotional Intelligence Assessment

To start enhancing your emotional intelligence, it's helpful to know your starting point. Several tools and assessments can provide insights into your emotional intelligence strengths and areas for growth.

Resources for Assessing Emotional Intelligence:

- **The Emotional Intelligence Appraisal**: This assessment, based on the work of Travis Bradberry and Jean Greaves, measures your emotional intelligence in four domains: self-awareness, self-management, social awareness, and relationship management.

- **The Mayer-Salovey-Caruso Emotional Intelligence Test (MSCEIT)**: Developed by the pioneers of EI research, this test assesses your ability to perceive, use, understand, and manage emotions.

Remember, these assessments are tools for self-discovery, not definitive judgments of your character. Use them to identify areas for growth and to track your progress over time.

In nurturing our emotional intelligence, we equip ourselves with the tools needed for more meaningful and satisfying interactions. By understanding and managing our emotions, we pave the way for deeper connections with others, enriching our lives and the lives of those around us.

2.1 Empathy: The Key to Truly Understanding Others

Empathy, in its essence, represents our ability to sense and understand the emotions of those around us, a crucial factor in forging genuine human connections. It can be broken down into cognitive, emotional, and compassionate components, each playing a distinct role in our interactions.

Cognitive empathy refers to our capacity to understand another person's perspective or mental state. It's the intellectual aspect of empathy that allows us to recognize what another person might be thinking in a given situation. Emotional empathy, on the other hand, is the ability to physically feel the emotions of another as if they were our own. This type of empathy can create a deep sense of connection but can also be overwhelming if not managed properly. Compassionate empathy goes beyond merely understanding or sharing another's feelings; it compels us to take action, to help however we can.

Cultivating empathy involves more than just a willingness to connect with others; it requires active effort and practice. Here are a few strategies that can enhance your empathic skills:

- Practice active listening: Focus fully on the speaker, acknowledge their feelings, and provide feedback that shows you've understood their message. This not only helps in comprehending their emotional state but also makes the speaker feel valued and heard.

- Engage in perspective-taking: Try to see situations from the other person's viewpoint. This can involve imagining yourself in their position or asking questions to gain insight into their experiences and feelings.

- Emotional mirroring: Reflect the emotions you're observing in others. This doesn't mean you should fake emotions but rather allow yourself to be genuinely moved by another's emotional state.

- Be curious about others: Show genuine interest in the lives of those around you. Ask open-ended questions that encourage them to share more about their feelings and experiences.

Empathy in action can lead to transformative outcomes in both personal and professional realms. Consider a manager who notices a team member's performance declining. By employing empathy, the manager can understand the challenges the employee is facing, perhaps related to stress or personal issues, and offer support or adjustments to their workload. This not only aids the employee but can also prevent further issues and foster a supportive workplace culture.

However, cultivating empathy is not without its challenges. Biases, whether based on race, gender, age, or other factors, can cloud our ability to empathize equally with all individuals. Emotional burnout is another risk, particularly for those in caregiving roles, where constant empathizing can lead to emotional exhaustion.

To overcome these barriers, consider the following:

- Acknowledge and confront personal biases: Reflect on your preconceptions about people and consider how they might affect your ability to empathize. Actively seek to broaden your perspectives by engaging with diverse groups and viewpoints.

- Set emotional boundaries: While empathy allows us to share in the feelings of others, it's important to maintain a boundary that prevents these emotions from overwhelming us. Techniques such as mindfulness can help in managing our emotional investment.

- Seek support: For those in roles that involve high levels of emotional labor, finding a support network or professional help can provide an outlet for the stresses and strains of empathic engagement.

In our fast-paced world, where genuine connections can sometimes feel fleeting, empathy emerges as a beacon of hope. It reminds us of the power of understanding, the strength found in shared emotions, and the profound impact compassion can have on the world around us. Through empathy, we find not only a pathway to deeper connections but also a means to enrich our lives and the lives of those we touch.

2.2 Emotional Contagion: How Feelings Spread in Social Interactions

Emotional contagion, a term that might evoke images of a cold spreading through an office, is similarly about the transmission of emotions from one person to another, albeit far less visible and often subconsciously enacted. It's the reason behind a room's shift in mood when someone brings either a spark of enthusiasm or a cloud of gloom into it. This phenomenon is grounded in our inherent social nature, which drives us to synchronize our emotions with those around us, creating a shared emotional experience.

The Phenomenon of Emotional Contagion

Understanding emotional contagion begins with recognizing that humans are wired for empathy; we naturally tune into the emotions of those around us, often without conscious effort. This tuning in allows emotions to 'jump' from person to person, influencing feelings and behaviors in a ripple effect. For instance, a leader's positivity can inspire an entire team, just as a family member's anxiety can unsettle the household. This automatic mimicry of emotions serves as a social glue, bonding individuals through shared experiences and ensuring harmonious interactions.

Mechanisms of Transmission

The pathways through which emotions are transmitted are primarily non-verbal. Our brains are adept at picking up and mimicking subtle cues such as facial expressions, tone of voice, posture, and even breathing patterns. This mimicry happens in the blink of an eye, with the observer often unconsciously adopting the emotional state of the observed. For example, witnessing a friend's genuine smile can trigger an automatic smile response, a direct link to feeling happier. Similarly, observing someone's slumped posture and downcast gaze can lead to a mirroring of those cues, pulling our mood down.

To grasp the depth of these mechanisms, consider the following:

- Facial expressions are powerful conveyors of emotion, often elicited and recognized universally across different cultures.

- Vocal tones carry emotional timbres, with variations in pitch, pace, and volume offering clues to the speaker's emotional state.

- Gestures and postures can communicate a wide range of feelings, from confidence and openness to anxiety and defensiveness.

Harnessing Emotional Contagion

While the automatic nature of emotional contagion might suggest a lack of control, we can indeed influence the process, using it to foster positive environments:

- Leaders can model emotional resilience and optimism, setting a tone that encourages a constructive and supportive team dynamic.

- In group settings, consciously maintaining a positive demeanor can uplift the collective mood, making collaborative efforts more enjoyable and productive.

- Educators can leverage emotional contagion to create an engaging and motivating learning atmosphere, captivating students' interest and facilitating deeper understanding.

Strategies to harness emotional contagion include:

- Being mindful of one's emotional state before entering social situations, preparing to project emotions that will positively influence the group.

- Using body language deliberately to convey positive emotions, such as maintaining open postures and making eye contact.

- Employing humor and shared laughter as a tool to elevate the mood and cohesiveness of a group.

Guarding Against Negative Spillover

Protecting oneself from the negative spillover of others' emotions is equally important. This involves setting emotional boundaries and developing skills to maintain one's emotional equilibrium:

- Practice mindfulness to enhance awareness of your emotional state, enabling you to recognize when you're beginning to absorb the negative emotions of others.

- Develop techniques to detach and decompress, such as focused breathing or brief meditation, to reset your emotional state.

- Cultivate a support network of friends or colleagues who understand the challenges of emotional contagion and can offer perspective and reassurance when needed.

In moments where negative emotions are pervasive:

- Acknowledge the emotions present without immediately adopting them, allowing for a conscious choice in how to respond.

- Seek to understand the root cause of the negative emotions in others, which can provide insights into how best to offer support or address underlying issues.

- When appropriate, redirect conversations towards solutions or positive perspectives, helping shift the emotional tone of the interaction.

Understanding and managing emotional contagion is a nuanced journey, one that requires attention, practice, and a keen sense of empathy. By acknowledging the power of our emotions to influence those around us, we open the door to creating environments that are not only more emotionally intelligent but also more nurturing and productive. The ability to harness this phenomenon for positive outcomes, while protecting oneself from negative influences, is a valuable skill in building deeper connections and fostering a sense of shared humanity.

2.3 Managing Emotions in Others: Strategies for Diffusing Conflict

In the realm of human interactions, conflicts are as inevitable as the rising and setting of the sun. They stem from differences in perspectives, needs, and values. Yet, it's not the presence of conflict that shapes our relationships, but how we navigate through these turbulent waters. A crucial aspect of this navigation involves managing emotions—ours and those of others. This part of the chapter will explore techniques for identifying emotional triggers, effective communication strategies for calming heightened emotions, the critical role of emotional intelligence in resolving conflicts, and practical scenarios with solutions for common conflicts in various environments.

Recognizing Emotional Triggers

To adeptly manage emotions in others, the first step is identifying what sparks these emotions. Emotional triggers are specific topics, situations, or behaviors that elicit strong emotional responses. These can vary widely among individuals, with common triggers including feeling disrespected, unheard, or undervalued. Recognizing these triggers involves:

- Attentive Listening: Paying close attention to what is being said, how it's being said, and what is left unsaid. Changes in tone, pace, or volume can indicate an emotional shift.

- Observing Non-verbal Cues: Body language such as crossed arms, avoidance of eye contact, or fidgeting can signal discomfort or agitation.

- Understanding the Individual: Familiarity with a person's background, values, and past experiences can provide insights into potential triggers.

Communication Techniques

Once triggers are identified, employing effective communication techniques can help in de-escalating emotions. Key strategies include:

- Validating Feelings: Acknowledge the other person's emotions without judgment. Statements like "I can see why that would be upsetting" can validate their feelings, making them more receptive to dialogue.

- Reflective Listening: Paraphrase what the other person has said to ensure understanding. This not only clarifies any miscommunications but also shows that you are engaged and value their perspective.

- Calm and Clear Expression: Use a calm tone and clear language to express your thoughts and feelings. Avoid accusatory phrases, opting instead for "I" statements that focus on how you perceive the situation without placing blame.

- Offering Solutions: Instead of dwelling on the problem, shift the focus to potential solutions. Encourage collaborative problem-solving by asking for the other person's input and preferences.

Role of Emotional Intelligence

Emotional intelligence plays a pivotal role in conflict resolution and negotiation. It enables us to:

- Stay Composed: High emotional intelligence allows for better control over our emotions, preventing them from escalating the conflict.

- Empathize: Understanding the emotions behind the other person's actions or words can change the course of the conflict, opening pathways to resolution that respect both parties' needs and feelings.

- Navigate Emotions: Emotional intelligence helps in navigating not only our emotions but also in identifying the emotional landscape of the conflict, allowing for more targeted and effective solutions.

Practical Conflict Resolution Scenarios

Let's explore examples of common conflict scenarios and how emotional intelligence can guide us to resolution:

- **Workplace Disagreement**: Two team members argue over the direction of a project. Recognizing the trigger as a fear of undervaluation, the team leader validates both perspectives and facilitates a meeting where each member can present their views calmly. Using reflective listening, the leader ensures both parties feel heard, steering them towards a compromise that aligns with the project's goals.

- **Family Conflict**: A parent and teenager clash over curfew times. The parent identifies the trigger as the teenager's need for independence. By expressing their concerns calmly and inviting the teenager to suggest a compromise, they reach an agreement that considers both the teenager's desire for autonomy and the parent's concern for safety.

- **Friendship Strain**: Miscommunication leads to hurt feelings between friends. Recognizing the emotional trigger as feeling disrespected, one friend initiates a conversation to clarify the misunderstanding. Through validating feelings and reflective listening, they clear up the miscommunication and reaffirm their appreciation for each other.

In each scenario, the resolution hinges on recognizing emotional triggers, employing empathetic and clear communication, and leveraging emotional intelligence to navigate the emotions involved. This approach not only diffuses the immediate conflict but also strengthens the underlying relationship, building a foundation of mutual respect and understanding that can weather future storms.

2.4 The Role of Emotional Intelligence in Leadership and Influence

In the realm of leadership, emotional intelligence emerges not as an optional virtue but as a foundational element driving effective leadership and profound influence. It is the undercurrent that enables leaders to navigate the complexities of human dynamics, inspire collective action, and foster environments where individuals feel valued and understood. This segment reveals how emotional intelligence acts as a catalyst for leadership success, offering insights into its development, application in influencing others, and strategies for cultivating resilient teams.

Emotional intelligence equips leaders with the insight to recognize not only their emotions but also those of their team members. It allows them to understand the impact of these emotions on the team's dynamics and performance. Developing this form of intelligence involves a commitment to ongoing self-reflection, seeking feedback, and engaging in activities that enhance one's ability to empathize, regulate emotions, and navigate social interactions adeptly.

Influencing others through emotional intelligence involves a nuanced approach where leaders use their understanding of emotions to motivate and connect with their teams. This influence is not about manipulation but about genuine connection and inspiration. For example, a leader aware of their team's apprehensions about a new project might use this understanding to address concerns directly, offer support, and highlight the project's benefits in a way that resonates with the team's values and aspirations. Such an approach not only alleviates concerns but also cultivates a sense of shared purpose and motivation.

Building resilient teams is another area where emotional intelligence plays a pivotal role. Resilient teams are characterized by their ability to navigate challenges, adapt to changes, and support one another through setbacks. Leaders can foster this resilience by:

- Encouraging open communication: Creating an environment where team members feel comfortable sharing their thoughts, feelings, and concerns without fear of judgment.

- Promoting empathy and understanding: Encouraging team members to consider their colleagues' perspectives and challenges, fostering a supportive and cohesive team dynamic.

- Leading by example: Demonstrating resilience in the face of challenges, showing that setbacks are opportunities for learning and growth.

Real-world examples further illustrate the transformative power of emotional intelligence in leadership. Consider the case of a non-profit organization facing significant funding cuts. The director, recognizing the team's anxiety, shared her concerns and outlined a clear plan to navigate the financial challenges. By doing so, she not only validated the team's feelings but also inspired confidence in their collective ability to overcome the obstacles. Her emotional intelligence—specifically, her ability to empathize with her team's concerns and communicate a vision for the future—played a crucial role in maintaining team morale and focus during a difficult period.

Another example is a tech company where the CEO implemented regular feedback sessions designed to understand employees' aspirations, concerns, and ideas for improvement. This initiative, driven by the CEO's commitment to emotional intelligence, led to significant improvements in employee satisfaction and innovation. The CEO's ability to listen, empathize, and act on feedback demonstrated a leadership style deeply influenced by emotional intelligence, resulting in a more motivated and engaged workforce.

As these examples show, emotional intelligence is not merely an abstract concept but a practical tool that leaders can develop and apply to achieve remarkable outcomes. It is the bridge that connects individual aspirations with collective goals, transforming the workplace into a space where people feel understood, valued, and motivated to contribute their best.

In closing, the journey through emotional intelligence in leadership reveals its critical role in shaping leaders who are not just effective but also deeply influential and capable of building resilient teams. This exploration underscores the importance of emotional intelligence as a skill that leaders can develop and refine to inspire, motivate, and lead with empathy and understanding. As we move forward, the insights gained from this segment serve as a foundation for navigating the complexities of human interactions, whether in leadership roles or in our everyday lives. The principles of emotional intelligence outlined here pave the way for more meaningful connections, enhanced personal growth, and the realization of collective aspirations.

CHAPTER 3

The Mechanics Behind Motivation and Behavior

Imagine you're at a crossroads, one path paved with gold, the other, a simple dirt road, yet it's the one that makes your heart race. This moment encapsulates the essence of human motivation— a force so powerful it can drive us to choose passion over profit, challenge over comfort. In this chapter, we delve into the complex interplay of needs, desires, and motivations that guide our behaviors and influence our interactions with others. By understanding these underlying mechanisms, we unlock the ability to predict behavior, foster deeper connections, and navigate social landscapes with nuanced insight.

Understanding Maslow's Hierarchy

Abraham Maslow's hierarchy of needs is a psychological theory that categorizes human needs into a five-tier model, often depicted as a pyramid. At the base are physiological needs, like food and shelter, followed by safety needs, love and belonging, esteem, and, at the pinnacle, self-actualization. Maslow posited that lower-level needs must be satisfied before individuals can attend to higher-level needs.

In real-world terms, consider a student struggling with financial instability; their focus is likely on securing part-time work (safety needs) rather than joining a social club (love and belonging) or excelling in extracurricular activities (esteem and self-actualization). This model helps us understand the motivations behind people's actions and the importance of addressing fundamental needs before higher-level growth can occur.

Intrinsic vs. Extrinsic Motivation

Diving deeper into what drives us, motivation is often categorized into two types: intrinsic and extrinsic. Intrinsic motivation comes from within, driven by personal satisfaction or the joy of doing something. For example, a writer may pen stories because they love crafting narratives, not for fame or financial gain. Extrinsic motivation, on the other hand, is fueled by external rewards or pressures, like working overtime for a bonus or studying hard to avoid parental disapproval.

Understanding the balance between intrinsic and extrinsic motivations in individuals can significantly impact how we interact and communicate with them. For instance, praising a child's effort and enjoyment in playing piano (intrinsic) rather than solely their success in a recital (extrinsic) can nurture a lifelong love for music over a fleeting desire for accolades.

Application in Reading People

Recognizing someone's motivations can be a game-changer in predicting their behavior. A manager, by identifying an employee's intrinsic motivation for creativity, might assign them to a project designing a new marketing campaign, tapping into their passion and likely boosting their productivity and satisfaction. In contrast, an employee motivated extrinsically by career advancement may thrive when given clear, achievement-oriented goals and recognition for their successes.

This understanding can also transform interpersonal relationships. When we acknowledge our friend's intrinsic motivation for adventure and suggest a spontaneous road trip, we strengthen our bond by aligning with their core desires.

Motivation in Various Contexts

Motivations can shift dramatically across different areas of our lives and are further influenced by cultural contexts. In professional settings, extrinsic motivations like salary and job title often play significant roles, but intrinsic motivations related to personal growth and job satisfaction are crucial drivers of long-term engagement and success.

Cultural influences can also shape motivation. In collectivist cultures, where community and family ties are emphasized, motivations may lean towards fulfilling familial expectations or contributing to community wellbeing. Conversely, in individualistic cultures, personal achievement and self-expression may be more significant motivators.

Understanding these nuances allows us to navigate social interactions more effectively, tailoring our approach to align with the diverse motivations of those around us. Whether in a professional setting, within our personal relationships, or when interacting with individuals from different cultural backgrounds, an awareness of the underlying motivations can guide our interactions towards more meaningful and productive outcomes.

In this exploration of human motivation, from the foundational needs described by Maslow to the intricate dance between intrinsic and extrinsic drivers, we uncover the forces that propel us forward, shape our decisions, and color our world. By applying these insights, we not only predict behavior with greater accuracy but also cultivate deeper, more empathetic connections with those around us.

3.1 Personality Types and Behavior Patterns: Predicting Reactions

Personality shapes the tapestry of human behavior in nuanced and profound ways. It influences how we perceive the world, interact with others, and make decisions. A deeper understanding of personality theories and their application can significantly enhance our ability to anticipate reactions and tailor our communication strategies effectively.

Personality Theories

At the heart of personality psychology lies a quest to categorize and understand the diverse range of human behaviors and traits. Among the various models developed over the years, the Big Five personality traits stand out for their empirical support and widespread acceptance. This model posits that five broad dimensions encapsulate most of the significant variation in human personality: Openness, Conscientiousness, Extraversion, Agreeableness, and Neuroticism (OCEAN).

- **Openness** involves appreciation for art, emotion, adventure, unusual ideas, curiosity, and variety of experience.

- **Conscientiousness** reflects a tendency to show self-discipline, act dutifully, and aim for achievement against measures or outside expectations.

- **Extraversion** indicates how outgoing and social a person is.

- **Agreeableness** shows a tendency toward compassion and cooperation rather than suspicion and antagonism.

- **Neuroticism** refers to the degree of emotional stability and impulse control and is sometimes referred to inversely as Emotional Stability.

Understanding these dimensions provides a framework for predicting how individuals might behave in different scenarios and tailoring interaction strategies to align with their personality traits.

Personality Assessments

Various tools and assessments have been developed to measure the Big Five traits, offering insights into individual personalities. These assessments, such as the NEO Personality Inventory or the Five-Factor Model, provide scores for each of the five traits, offering a snapshot of an individual's personality profile.

While these tools can be valuable in understanding personality, they come with limitations. Results can be influenced by the respondent's mood at the time of taking the test or their level of self-awareness. Additionally, these assessments provide general tendencies rather than definitive predictions of behavior. Therefore, they should be used as guides rather than absolute indicators of personality.

Predicting Behavior Based on Personality

Armed with an understanding of the Big Five traits, we can begin to anticipate how individuals might react in various situations. For instance:

- An individual scoring high on **Openness** might be more receptive to new ideas and unconventional approaches, making them ideal candidates for roles that require creativity and innovation.

- Someone who scores high on **Conscientiousness** may prefer structured tasks and detailed planning, thriving in environments where precision and organization are valued.

- A person with high **Extraversion** might excel in social situations, making them natural leaders or salespeople, where their ability to connect with others can be leveraged.

- High **Agreeableness** suggests a preference for harmony and collaboration, indicating that such individuals might be effective in roles that require teamwork and mediation.

- Understanding that a person with high **Neuroticism** might be more sensitive to stress can help in providing support and creating a work environment that minimizes unnecessary pressures.

Adapting Interaction Strategies

Leveraging insights from personality assessments allows for more personalized and effective communication. Here are strategies to consider:

- For those high in **Openness**, present ideas in a way that emphasizes novelty and creativity. Encourage their input on innovative solutions and value their unconventional perspectives.

- When interacting with someone high in **Conscientiousness**, respect their need for order and reliability. Be punctual, organized, and clear in your expectations.

- Engaging with highly **Extraverted** individuals, provide opportunities for them to express themselves and take the lead in discussions. They appreciate being in vibrant, energetic settings.

- With people high in **Agreeableness**, emphasize collaboration and consensus. They respond well to a cooperative approach and appreciate efforts to maintain positive relationships.

- In dealing with those who have high **Neuroticism**, strive to create a stable, supportive environment. Offer reassurances, and be patient and understanding of their concerns.

By applying these tailored strategies, we foster more meaningful connections and smoother interactions, whether in personal relationships, professional environments, or casual encounters. Recognizing and respecting personality differences not only enhances our ability to communicate effectively but also enriches our understanding of the complex mosaic of human behavior.

3.2 The Impact of Cognitive Biases on Perception and Judgment

Our minds, marvelous as they are, come with their own set of pre-installed filters—cognitive biases that shape the way we see the world and interpret the actions of others. These biases, often subconscious, can significantly influence our perception and judgment, leading us down a path of misunderstanding and misinterpretation.

Identifying Common Cognitive Biases

Several cognitive biases play pivotal roles in how we perceive and judge others:

- **Confirmation Bias**: The tendency to search for, interpret, favor, and recall information in a way that confirms one's preexisting beliefs or hypotheses.

- **Fundamental Attribution Error**: The inclination to attribute others' actions to their character or personality, while attributing our own behaviors to situational factors.

- **Halo Effect**: The phenomenon where a positive impression of a person in one area influences our judgment of their character and abilities in other areas.

- **Groupthink**: The practice of thinking or making decisions as a group in a way that discourages creativity or individual responsibility.

Understanding these biases is the first step towards mitigating their influence on our judgment and interactions.

Biases in Reading People

Cognitive biases can significantly distort our understanding of others' behaviors and intentions. For instance, confirmation bias might lead us to overlook evidence that contradicts our initial impression of someone. We may also misjudge someone's actions through the lens of the fundamental attribution error, attributing their mistake to a lack of effort or skill rather than considering external pressures they might be facing. These biases can cloud our judgment, leading to misunderstandings and potentially damaging relationships.

Mitigating Bias

Awareness is crucial in counteracting the effects of cognitive biases. Here are strategies to help recognize and mitigate bias in our judgments:

- **Seek Contrary Evidence**: Actively look for information that challenges your initial impressions or beliefs about someone. This can help counteract confirmation bias and ensure a more balanced view.

- **Consider the Context**: Remind yourself to consider situational factors that may be influencing someone's behavior. This can help reduce the impact of the fundamental attribution error.

- **Encourage Diverse Perspectives**: Surround yourself with a variety of viewpoints. Engaging with people who see the world differently can help challenge your assumptions and reduce groupthink.

- **Question First Impressions**: Be mindful that first impressions, while powerful, are not always accurate. Allow for the possibility that your initial judgment may be influenced by the halo effect and may need revisiting.

Critical Thinking Skills

Developing critical thinking skills is essential in navigating the complexities of human behavior and relationships. Critical thinking involves analyzing facts to form a judgment, free as much as possible from the influence of personal bias. It requires:

- **Active Questioning**: Don't take things at face value. Ask questions that probe deeper into the reasons behind someone's actions or decisions.

- **Reflective Thinking**: Spend time reflecting on your own thought processes. Consider why you think the way you do about a person or situation and whether your judgments are based on solid evidence or biased thinking.

- **Open-mindedness**: Be willing to change your opinion in the light of new, credible evidence. Cultivating an attitude of open-mindedness supports a more flexible and accurate understanding of others.

By employing these techniques, we can sharpen our critical thinking skills, allowing us to see beyond the surface and appreciate the complex tapestry of human motivation and behavior. This not only aids in making more informed judgments about others but also enriches our interactions, fostering connections that are rooted in understanding and respect.

As we navigate our social worlds, being mindful of the biases that color our perceptions and judgments is crucial. By actively working to mitigate these biases and employing critical thinking, we open ourselves up to a richer, more nuanced understanding of those around us. This awareness not only enhances our interpersonal relationships but also allows us to move through the world with a more open and inquisitive mindset.

3.3 Psychological Theories Behind Lying and Deception

In the intricate dance of human interaction, lying and deception play roles that are as complex as they are controversial. At one point or another, we all find ourselves weaving tales not wholly rooted in reality, whether to protect someone's feelings, to avoid unwanted consequences, or to navigate socially awkward situations. This section explores the psychological underpinnings of why we choose to depart from the truth, the subtle signs that betray our deceit, the profound impact of lies on the foundation of trust, and the ethical dilemmas we face in uncovering and handling deceit.

Why People Lie

The act of lying is a testament to our cognitive complexity. Psychologists pinpoint several motivations behind why individuals resort to deception:

- **Self-Protection**: Avoiding punishment or negative outcomes is a primary driver. This can range from a child denying their involvement in a broken vase to an employee obscuring a mistake at work.

- **Benefit Seeking**: Gaining rewards not otherwise attainable if the truth were known, such as embellishing a resume to secure a job.

- **Altruistic Reasons**: Protecting others from harm or discomfort, often termed 'white lies'. An example is complimenting a friend's cooking despite finding it unpalatable, to avoid hurting their feelings.

- **Self-Enhancement**: Boosting one's image or status, such as exaggerating achievements to appear more competent or successful.

- **Pathological Lying**: For some, lying becomes compulsive, not necessarily tied to any of the above motivations but stemming from a deeper psychological need.

Detecting Lies

While the motivations for lying vary widely, so do the cues that might indicate deception. Despite popular belief, no single sign conclusively points to a lie. However, a cluster of non-verbal cues can raise suspicion:

- **Facial Inconsistencies**: A forced smile not reaching the eyes, rapid blinking, or fleeting expressions of fear or guilt can suggest discomfort with the truth.

- **Body Language**: Fidgeting, self-touching gestures like rubbing the neck or face, and the use of physical barriers like crossing arms may indicate deceit.

- **Verbal Cues**: Hesitations in speech, unnecessary details, and inconsistencies in storytelling can be red flags.

- **Vocal Characteristics**: Changes in pitch, speaking rate, and throat clearing are often observed in deceptive individuals.

Yet, it's crucial to remember that these indicators are not foolproof; stress, nervousness, or cultural differences can also prompt such behaviors.

The Psychology of Trust

Trust, the bedrock of all human relationships, can be significantly affected by lies. Trust is built through consistent, honest interactions, creating a sense of predictability and safety. When lies are discovered, they shatter this foundation, leading to feelings of betrayal and uncertainty. Rebuilding trust requires time, transparency, and a commitment to honesty, often more challenging than establishing it initially.

The dynamics of trust and deception highlight the delicate balance in relationships. On one hand, complete honesty without tact can harm just as much as deceit. On the other, lies, even when well-intentioned, can erode trust if they become known. Navigating this landscape requires a nuanced understanding of both the value of truth and the potential consequences of deception.

Ethical Considerations

The realm of lying and deception also brings us face to face with ethical considerations, especially when it comes to detecting and confronting lies. Ethical dilemmas arise in questions such as:

- **Is it right to expose a lie if doing so would cause harm?**

- **What are the responsibilities of someone who detects deceit?**

- **How do we balance the need for honesty with the potential for negative repercussions?**

In professional settings, such as law enforcement or therapy, these questions become even more complex. Professionals must weigh the benefits of uncovering the truth against the ethical obligation to respect privacy and maintain confidentiality.

Ethics also come into play in our personal lives. Deciding whether to confront a friend or family member about a suspected lie involves considering the potential impact on the relationship. Is the truth worth the possible fallout? Or is it better to approach the situation with empathy, seeking to understand the motivations behind the deception?

In conclusion, lying and deception are multifaceted aspects of human behavior, woven into the very fabric of our interactions. Understanding the psychological reasons behind why people lie, recognizing the signs of deception, grappling with the impact on trust, and navigating the ethical landscape of uncovering lies are all crucial in fostering healthy, honest relationships. As we navigate these waters, we are reminded of the complexity of human nature and the importance of empathy, understanding, and ethical consideration in all our interactions.

3.4 Trust and Mistrust: Signs and Signals in Building Relationships

The fabric of our relationships, both personal and professional, is woven with threads of trust. This invisible yet palpable force is what allows people to feel safe, to open up, and to invest in one another. But what lays the foundation for trust to flourish, and how can we detect its presence or absence through non-verbal communication? More importantly, when trust is damaged, what steps can we take towards its restoration? This section explores these questions, providing insights into the complex dynamics of trust.

Foundations of Trust

At the heart of any trusting relationship is a blend of reliability, honesty, and emotional safety. These elements act as the pillars supporting the weight of our shared experiences and expectations. For trust to take root:

- **Reliability** must be consistent. Actions and words need to align over time, proving predictability and dependability.

- **Honesty** should be evident. Transparency in communication and behavior fosters a sense of integrity.

- **Emotional safety** is crucial. Knowing one can express thoughts and feelings without fear of judgment or reprisal engenders a deeper sense of security.

Non-Verbal Cues of Trustworthiness

Our bodies often speak volumes more than our words, sending signals about our trustworthiness or the lack thereof. Some of these cues include:

- **Eye contact**: Maintaining a steady gaze conveys sincerity, while shifty eyes might suggest discomfort or deceit.

- **Open posture**: When we face someone directly, with arms uncrossed and palms visible, it signals openness and willingness to connect.

- **Mirroring**: Subtly mimicking the other person's posture or gestures can indicate empathy and alignment, strengthening the bond.

- **Proximity and touch**: Leaning in during conversation or appropriate, gentle touches can demonstrate care and affirm trust.

Rebuilding Trust

Restoring trust is a delicate process, requiring time, patience, and concerted effort from both parties. Steps towards reconciliation include:

- **Acknowledgment of hurt**: The party that breached the trust must recognize and validate the pain caused.

- **Sincere apology**: A genuine expression of remorse, acknowledging the wrongdoing and its impact, is essential.

- **Transparent communication**: Openly discussing the breakdown and how to prevent future occurrences helps rebuild trust.

- **Consistent behavior**: Actions that consistently match words over time will gradually restore trust.

Case Studies on Trust

Real-life scenarios underscore the pivotal role trust plays in outcomes. For instance, a startup's success hinged on the trust between its co-founders. Initially, miscommunications and unmet expectations eroded their trust, leading to conflicts. However, through open dialogue, acknowledgment of each other's concerns, and a commitment to transparency, they rebuilt their partnership, steering their startup to new heights.

In another case, a long-term friendship was tested when one friend failed to support the other during a crisis. The aggrieved party expressed their feelings of betrayal, leading to an honest conversation about expectations and boundaries. Over time, through consistent efforts to be present and supportive, trust was mended, and the friendship emerged stronger.

These examples illustrate that trust is both the foundation and the glue of meaningful relationships. It demands our attention, care, and respect to grow and sustain.

As we wrap up this exploration of trust and mistrust, it's clear that the journey of building, maintaining, and sometimes repairing trust is integral to the depth and durability of our relationships. Trust acts as the compass guiding our interactions, influencing our openness to connect, share, and invest in one another. Through understanding the signs of trust, recognizing its foundational elements, and embracing the path to its restoration, we enhance our capacity for meaningful connections. This understanding not only enriches our current relationships but also prepares us for the complexities of those we have yet to form.

Moving forward, the insights garnered here serve as a beacon, illuminating the nuances of human behavior and interaction. They underscore the profound impact of trust on the dynamics of our relationships, highlighting its role as a critical element in the tapestry of human connection. As we continue on this journey, let us carry forward the lessons learned, applying them to foster deeper, more resilient bonds with those around us.

CHAPTER 4

Reading Between the Pixels: Unveiling Digital Body Language

In an age where screens serve as windows to our souls, the digital footprints we leave behind—be it through emails, texts, or social media posts—carry the essence of our emotions, thoughts, and behaviors. Each tap, type, and swipe is a reflection of our inner selves, translated into pixels and data. This chapter peels back the layers of digital interactions, revealing how the subtleties of our online communications provide a wealth of understanding about who we are and how we relate to the world around us.

Digital Expressions

The digital realm is rich with expressions of our identity and emotions. From the emojis we select to punctuate our messages to the hashtags we use to categorize our thoughts, every choice is a piece of the puzzle of our digital persona. Consider the difference in tone between a text punctuated with a smiley face versus one with a period. The former radiates warmth and approachability, while the latter, though possibly unintentional, may come across as cold or final.

- **Photos and Videos**: The images we share tell stories of what we value, fear, love, and aspire to be. A profile filled with nature shots might hint at a love for the outdoors or a desire for peace, while a feed dominated by selfies could suggest a focus on self-image or a cry for validation.

- **Likes, Shares, and Comments**: These actions form a non-verbal chorus of agreement, dissent, or solidarity. A post that garners significant interaction becomes a beacon of shared values or interests, creating a digital echo chamber of like-minded individuals.

Analyzing Writing Styles

The way we compose our digital communications—our choice of words, the structure of our sentences, and even our punctuation—can reveal much about our emotional state and intentions. Writing style serves as a mirror to our mood; a hurriedly composed email full of typos might indicate stress or distraction, whereas a message crafted with careful consideration and rich vocabulary could reflect a calm and thoughtful state of mind.

- **Timing and Frequency**: The urgency or delay in our responses also speaks volumes. A rapid reply can signal eagerness or availability, while delayed responses might suggest busyness, disinterest, or the need for careful thought before responding.

- **Capitals and Emphasis**: The use of ALL CAPS, bold, or italics often signifies strong emotion, be it excitement, anger, or emphasis, translating vocal inflections into visual cues.

Emotional Leakage in Digital Communication

Even in the seemingly neutral territory of emails or texts, our emotions find ways to seep through. This "emotional leakage" can be as subtle as the choice of a sign-off in an email—from the formal "Regards" to the more intimate "XOXO"—or as overt as the tone conveyed in a text message.

- **Word Choice and Sentiment**: Certain words carry emotional weight that can color a message with underlying feelings. Words like "unfortunately," "but," or "however" may introduce a negative sentiment, subtly altering the message's reception.

- **Punctuation**: The overuse or absence of punctuation marks can also hint at emotional states. Excessive exclamation points may convey excitement or intensity, while a lack of commas can make a message feel rushed or terse.

Privacy and Ethics

As we navigate the digital landscape, deciphering the hidden messages in our interactions, it's paramount to tread carefully, respecting the thin line between insight and intrusion. The ethical considerations of analyzing digital footprints are crucial:

- **Consent and Context**: Always consider the context of shared information and whether you have implicit permission to analyze it. Private messages or sensitive posts shared in confidence should be treated with the utmost respect and discretion.

- **Avoiding Assumptions**: While digital expressions can provide clues to a person's state of mind, they are not definitive proof of intent or emotion. It's essential to avoid jumping to conclusions based solely on digital interactions.

- **Respecting Boundaries**: Digital communication, for all its immediacy, often lacks the nuance of face-to-face interaction. Respecting individuals' boundaries and privacy online is as critical as it is in the physical world.

In conclusion, the digital realm offers a new dimension of understanding in the way we connect with one another. By paying attention to the subtleties of our online interactions, we gain insights into the emotional undercurrents that influence our digital expressions. However, wielding this knowledge responsibly, with empathy and respect for privacy, ensures that our exploration of digital body language enriches our connections rather than undermines them.

4.1 Video Calls: Reading Non-Verbal Cues Through the Screen

In today's world, video calls have become a staple of communication, bridging the gap between distance and time zones. However, the screen introduces unique challenges in reading non-verbal cues, an essential component of understanding and connecting with others. This section navigates the nuances of interpreting non-verbal communication in virtual settings, offering insights into enhancing empathy and rapport through screens.

Challenges of Digital Non-Verbal Reading

One primary obstacle in video calls is the limited visual field. Unlike in-person interactions where body posture, stance, and full-range gestures contribute to the conversation, video calls often restrict our view to faces and upper torsos. This truncation can make it challenging to gauge someone's full reaction or comfort level, as we miss out on the leg fidgets or the way someone might be tapping their foot anxiously.

Moreover, technical issues like lag or poor resolution can further obscure these cues, making it difficult to catch quick facial expressions or subtle shifts in demeanor. The digital medium also adds a layer of detachment; the warmth of a genuine smile or the energy of an enthusiastic nod might not translate as powerfully through a screen.

Key Cues in Virtual Settings

Despite these challenges, certain non-verbal cues remain potent indicators of emotions and intentions, even in digital conversations. Paying close attention to the following can enhance understanding:

- **Facial Expressions**: The human face can convey a myriad of emotions. On video calls, focus on the eyes and mouth. For instance, genuine smiles reach the eyes, crinkling them slightly, while polite smiles might not. Raised eyebrows can express surprise or concern, offering clues into the other person's reactions.

- **Gestures and Hand Movements**: Though the frame might be limited, hand movements can still provide insights. Open palms can indicate honesty and openness, while clenched fists might suggest frustration or anger. Observe how individuals use their hands to emphasize points or if they're hidden, possibly indicating nervousness.

- **Environmental Clues**: Backgrounds in video calls can offer context about a person's preferences, mood, or even their day. A cluttered space might suggest busyness or stress, while a carefully curated backdrop could indicate a desire to present a particular image or mood.

Enhancing Virtual Empathy

Developing empathy in video conferencing settings involves a mindful approach to interactions, acknowledging the inherent barriers while striving to connect deeply. Consider these strategies:

- **Active Engagement**: Show you're listening through nods and verbal affirmations. This active engagement helps bridge the emotional gap the digital medium might create.

- **Clarify Emotional States**: If you're unsure about someone's reaction due to the limitations of video calls, don't hesitate to ask. A simple "How does that make you feel?" can open the door to understanding their emotional state more clearly.

- **Personalize Your Space**: Make your background and setting more 'you'. This not only makes conversations more engaging but also gives others a glimpse into your world, fostering a deeper connection.

Practice Exercises

To sharpen your ability to read non-verbal cues through screens, engage in the following exercises:

- **Focused Observation**: During your next video call, dedicate a portion of your attention to observing non-verbal cues. After the call, jot down your observations and any emotions or intentions you inferred from them. Reflect on the accuracy of your interpretations by considering the context of the conversation.

- **Expressive Reading**: Partner with a friend or colleague for a video call where you both express specific emotions using only non-verbal cues. Attempt to guess each other's emotions. This exercise not only hones your observation skills but also highlights the expressive power of non-verbal communication, even in digital formats.

- **Background Analysis**: In a casual video call, invite participants to share stories or meanings behind one visible item in their background. This exercise not only adds a fun element to the call but also deepens your understanding of environmental clues.

Video calls, while presenting challenges for non-verbal communication, also offer a rich avenue for connection and understanding. By paying close attention to facial expressions, gestures, and environmental clues, and employing strategies to enhance empathy, we can navigate the digital divide, fostering meaningful interactions that resonate beyond the screen. Engaging in exercises to refine our observational skills ensures that we remain attuned to the subtleties of digital body language, enriching our virtual conversations with depth and empathy.

4.2 The Psychology of Online Interactions: Empathy in the Digital World

In the vast expanse of the internet, where words are our primary mode of connection, the ability to convey and interpret empathy becomes both a challenge and a necessity. The concept of digital empathy refers to our capacity to understand and share the feelings of others through online platforms. Its significance cannot be overstated, as it underpins the quality of our virtual interactions and relationships.

Digital Empathy

Digital empathy is the thread that weaves through the fabric of online communication, turning impersonal exchanges into meaningful connections. It involves recognizing emotions in written text, empathizing with the experiences shared in videos or posts, and responding in a way that communicates understanding and concern. However, without the cues available in face-to-face interactions, such as tone of voice or facial expressions, extending empathy online requires a heightened sense of awareness and intentionality.

- **Reading Between the Lines**: This entails paying close attention to the choice of words, emoji use, and overall tone of the message. Even without visual cues, messages often carry emotional undertones that can provide insights into the sender's state of mind.

- **Expressive Responses**: Using language that explicitly acknowledges the emotions being communicated by others. Phrases like "It sounds like you're feeling..." or "I can imagine that must have been hard for you" can convey empathy effectively.

Cultivating Compassion Online

The digital realm, with its anonymity and physical distance, can sometimes lead to a lack of compassion. Counteracting this involves deliberate efforts to humanize online interactions.

- **Personal Stories**: Sharing personal experiences can evoke empathy by highlighting common human struggles and victories. It makes abstract online personas more relatable and real.

- **Supportive Communities**: Participating in or creating online groups focused on mutual support, such as forums for specific challenges or interest-based groups, fosters a culture of compassion and understanding.

Overcoming Digital Dehumanization

A troubling aspect of online interactions is the tendency to dehumanize those we interact with, viewing them as mere avatars or usernames rather than complex individuals. This detachment can lead to harsher judgments and interactions than we might have in person.

- **Mindful Interaction**: Before posting or responding online, take a moment to consider the person on the other side of the screen. Reflect on how your words might affect them emotionally.

- **Challenge Negative Dynamics**: When witnessing dehumanization or negativity online, be a force for positivity. Offer words of support to the target or gently remind others of the human being behind the screen.

Building Digital Communities

Empathy plays a critical role in cultivating strong, supportive online communities. These spaces become havens where individuals feel seen, heard, and valued, encouraging open sharing and connection.

- **Inclusive Spaces**: Create forums or groups that welcome diverse perspectives and encourage members to share their experiences and emotions without fear of judgment.

- **Active Moderation**: Establish guidelines that promote respectful and empathetic interactions. Moderators can model this behavior and gently guide conversations to ensure a positive and supportive environment.

The digital world, vast and varied, holds incredible potential for connection and understanding. By prioritizing digital empathy in our online interactions, we contribute to a virtual landscape where compassion prevails, and genuine connections thrive. From the thoughtful construction of our messages to our engagement in digital communities, every action taken with empathy enriches the online experience, making it more human, more understanding, and infinitely more connected.

4.3 Navigating Digital Misunderstandings: A Guide for the Modern World

Misinterpretations in digital communication can twist the intended meaning of messages, leading to conflicts that could have been easily avoided. This section explores the labyrinth of digital misunderstandings, shedding light on their roots, and providing actionable advice to steer clear of them, or to mend the confusion they may cause.

Common Causes of Digital Misunderstandings

Several factors contribute to the maze of misunderstandings in digital interactions:

- **Lack of Context**: Text-based communication strips away the nuances of tone and body language, leaving much to be interpreted by the reader. This absence of context can distort the intended meaning.

- **Abbreviations and Slang**: The use of internet jargon, acronyms, and slang can confuse recipients unfamiliar with the terminology.

- **Cultural Differences**: Global digital communication brings together individuals from diverse backgrounds, where a phrase harmless in one culture could be offensive in another.

- **Emotional State of the Receiver**: The mood of the recipient at the time of reading a message can color their interpretation, turning neutral texts into perceived slights.

Clarification Techniques

When the message sent is not the message received, employing clarification techniques can help untangle the knots of confusion:

- **Restate Your Understanding**: Before reacting, summarize your interpretation of the message and ask for confirmation. This approach can uncover discrepancies in understanding without attributing blame.

- **Ask Open-Ended Questions**: Encourage elaboration by asking questions that cannot be answered with a simple 'yes' or 'no'. This invites the sender to provide more context, which can clarify their original message.

- **Use 'I' Statements**: Express how the message made you feel by starting sentences with 'I'. This reduces defensiveness and focuses on perception rather than accusation.

Digital Apologies

When misunderstandings occur, offering a sincere apology can smooth ruffled feathers and demonstrate your commitment to maintaining a positive relationship:

- **Timeliness**: Address the misunderstanding as soon as you become aware of it. Delaying an apology can imply indifference.

- **Sincerity**: A genuine apology acknowledges the misunderstanding and your role in it. Avoid phrases like "I'm sorry you felt that way," which can seem insincere.

- **Public vs. Private**: Consider the nature of the misunderstanding when deciding between a public or private apology. Public disputes might warrant a public apology, while misunderstandings in private communications are usually best addressed privately.

Preventive Strategies

Preventing misunderstandings before they happen can save time and preserve relationships. Here are some strategies to minimize confusion in digital communications:

- **Provide Context**: When initiating a conversation or making a request, include as much relevant information as possible. This helps prevent assumptions and fills in the gaps that non-verbal cues usually occupy.

- **Read Before Sending**: Take a moment to review your message from the recipient's perspective. This can help catch potentially confusing phrases or tones.

- **Set Expectations**: If you regularly communicate with the same individuals or groups, discuss and agree upon the meanings of commonly used phrases or acronyms to avoid future misunderstandings.

- **Cultural Sensitivity**: When communicating across cultures, take the time to learn about potential cultural differences that could impact interpretation. When in doubt, opt for clear and simple language.

- **Emotion Check**: Pause to assess your emotional state before responding to messages that spark strong reactions. If emotions are high, consider drafting your response and revisiting it later when you can view it more objectively.

Digital communication, for all its convenience, requires careful navigation to avoid the pitfalls of misunderstanding. By understanding the common causes and employing strategies for clarification, apology, and prevention, we can foster clearer, more effective online interactions. This not only helps in avoiding unnecessary conflicts but also strengthens our connections in a world where screens often stand between us.

4.4 Building Digital Rapport: Establishing Connections Online

Rapport in the digital realm is the bridge that links isolated islands in the vast sea of the internet, enabling individuals to traverse the gap between screens and miles. It's the glue that not only attracts but also binds people in the virtual world, turning fleeting interactions into lasting connections. This glue is not just about being liked; it's about creating a space where genuine interactions can flourish, fostering trust and understanding in an environment that often lacks the warmth of physical presence.

The Essentials of Digital Rapport

Digital rapport is the sense of connection and mutual understanding developed between individuals online. It's critical for virtual relationships because it lays the groundwork for meaningful interactions. Without it, conversations can feel impersonal and transient, lacking the depth that characterizes relationships in the physical world. Establishing rapport online involves recognizing the unique challenges and opportunities presented by digital communication and adapting strategies to overcome or leverage them.

Creating a Virtual Presence

Your digital presence is your ambassador in the online world, representing you in every interaction. Crafting this presence thoughtfully can significantly impact your ability to establish rapport:

- **Profile Optimization**: Use your profile to showcase aspects of your personality and interests. A well-chosen profile picture and a bio that reflects your sense of humor or passions can make you more relatable and approachable.

- **Consistency Across Platforms**: Maintain a consistent tone and style across different platforms. Whether you're more formal on LinkedIn and casual on Twitter, let your unique voice shine through in a way that's appropriate for each space.

Engagement Strategies

Engaging with others online in a way that builds rapport requires intention and adaptability. Here are strategies to consider:

- **Active Participation**: Don't just observe; contribute to discussions, share relevant content, and respond to comments. Your active involvement shows you're not just present but engaged and interested in the conversation.

- **Personalized Interactions**: Go beyond generic responses. Tailor your comments and messages to the individual, referencing past conversations or shared interests to demonstrate that you're paying attention.

- **Positivity and Support**: Encourage and uplift others with your posts and comments. A supportive word or a congratulatory message can go a long way in fostering positive feelings.

Maintaining Digital Relationships

Sustaining relationships over time in a digital context demands ongoing effort and the willingness to adapt to the evolving nature of online interactions:

- **Regular Check-ins**: Don't let too much time pass without reaching out. A simple message asking how someone is doing can keep the connection alive and show you care.

- **Shared Experiences**: Participate in virtual events, webinars, or online courses together. Shared experiences, even in the digital space, can strengthen bonds and provide new topics for conversation.

- **Adapting to Changes**: Be mindful of shifts in communication preferences and platforms. If a friend moves from Facebook to Instagram, follow suit to stay in touch in their preferred space.

In the expansive digital landscape, where interactions are mediated by technology, establishing and maintaining rapport is both an art and a science. It demands a blend of authenticity, consistency, and adaptability, allowing relationships to thrive despite the absence of physical proximity. By presenting ourselves thoughtfully, engaging with genuine interest, and nurturing our connections with care, we weave a web of relationships that enrich our digital lives and, by extension, our real-world experiences.

As we close this exploration of building digital rapport, we recognize its role as a cornerstone of virtual relationships. Crafting a presence that reflects our true selves, engaging with others in meaningful ways, and nurturing these connections over time are not just strategies for online interaction. They are essential components of forging deep, lasting relationships in an increasingly digital world. These principles guide us as we navigate the ever-evolving landscape of digital communication, reminding us of the power of connection in bridging the gap between the virtual and the tangible.

With this understanding, we turn our gaze to the horizon, eager to explore new dimensions of human interaction and the endless possibilities that await in the realm of digital communication.

CHAPTER 5

Signs of Deception: Unmasking the Truth

Imagine sitting across from someone as they share a story. Everything seems plausible, but something doesn't sit right with you. It's not just what they're saying but how they're saying it. Your intuition whispers, "Something's off." This feeling, often dismissed, is a crucial signal in detecting deception. In this digital age, where face-to-face interactions are increasingly replaced by screens, sharpening our ability to read these signals becomes not just useful but necessary.

Limitations of Traditional Lie Detection

Polygraphs, often showcased in crime dramas as the ultimate lie detectors, come with their own set of limitations. They measure physiological responses—heart rate, blood pressure, and sweat production—under the assumption that lying induces stress. However, these machines can't differentiate between the anxiety of lying and the nervousness of being tested. Furthermore, skilled individuals can manipulate their physiological responses to pass these tests, rendering the results unreliable.

Subtle Indicators of Deception

While no single cue conclusively indicates deception, a combination of subtle, non-verbal signals can raise suspicions. These include:

- **Incongruent Facial Expressions**: Genuine emotions are typically symmetrical and appear and disappear smoothly. Deceptive emotions might be asymmetrical or held for too long or too briefly.

- **Gestures that Don't Match Words**: When someone says "yes" but shakes their head no, this mismatch can be a red flag.

- **Touching the Face and Mouth**: This could indicate a subconscious attempt to "cover" the lie or the mouth.

- **Blink Rate**: Both increased blinking and prolonged eye closure can be indicators of deception, as they might signify an attempt to block out the observer or the discomfort of lying.

- **Foot Movement**: Nervousness can cause increased movement of the feet and legs. A deceptive person might shuffle their feet more, possibly as a physical manifestation of the desire to flee.

Contextual Analysis

Context plays a pivotal role in accurately interpreting potential signs of deceit. Consider the environment and the individual's baseline behavior. Someone might naturally avoid eye contact or touch their face often. Without understanding their normal behavior, these actions could be mistakenly read as deceptive. It's also essential to consider the stakes involved. High-stress situations, even without deception, can cause behaviors similar to those seen in lying, such as increased blinking or self-soothing gestures.

Practicing Discernment

Developing the ability to discern truth from deception requires practice and attention to detail. Here are exercises to hone this skill:

- **People Watching**: Spend time in a public place observing interactions. Note body language, facial expressions, and the context of the conversation. Guess the relationship between the people and the nature of their discussion. This practice sharpens observational skills.

- **Review Recorded Interactions**: Watch interviews or news segments with the sound off. Focus on the non-verbal cues and try to infer the emotional state of the speakers. Then, watch with sound to compare your observations with the actual content.

- **Baseline Behavior**: With friends or family, observe and note their common non-verbal cues in relaxed settings. This helps establish a baseline for their normal behavior, against which you can detect deviations in future interactions.

By integrating these practices into your routine, you'll gradually enhance your ability to detect subtle cues of deception. Yet, it's crucial to approach this skill with humility and an understanding of its limitations. Misreading signs can lead to false accusations and strained relationships. Therefore, while sharpening your observational skills, also cultivate empathy and open-mindedness. Remember, the goal is not to become a human lie detector but to improve your understanding of human behavior and interactions.

As we delve deeper into the nuances of detecting deception, it's clear that this skill, like any other, benefits from a balanced approach. Observing non-verbal cues, understanding the importance of context, and practicing discernment are steps toward more insightful and genuine interactions. While no method offers a foolproof way to unmask every lie, a careful and empathetic application of these techniques can significantly enhance our ability to navigate the complex web of human communication.

5.1 Trust-Building Techniques: Establishing Credibility and Reliability

In the intricate web of human relationships, trust acts as the cornerstone, influencing the depth and durability of our connections. This section shines a light on the pivotal strategies and practices that foster trust, focusing on the often-overlooked role of non-verbal communication, the pathway to mending broken trust, and real-life narratives that illustrate the transformative power of trust-building.

Foundations of Trust

Trust is not a commodity to be exchanged but a treasure to be cultivated, rooted in the fertile ground of consistency, integrity, and transparency. These elements, when nurtured, sprout the kind of trust that withstands the test of time and tribulation.

- **Consistency** is the rhythm that steadies the dance of human interactions, providing a predictable pattern that others can rely on. It's found in the small, repeated actions that, over time, create a solid foundation for trust.

- **Integrity** involves adhering to a set of principles, even when no one is watching. It's the moral compass that guides actions, ensuring they align with stated values and beliefs.

- **Transparency** is the willingness to be open and honest, sharing thoughts and intentions clearly. It removes the shroud of secrecy, allowing others to see and understand your genuine self.

Non-Verbal Signals of Trustworthiness

Words can build bridges or walls, but it's the silent language of our bodies that often speaks loudest about our trustworthiness. These non-verbal cues serve as powerful messengers, conveying sincerity, openness, and reliability.

- **Sustained Eye Contact** signals attention and respect, telling the other person they are valued and their words matter. It's a silent affirmation of engagement and interest.

- **Open Postures**, with arms relaxed and uncrossed, invite connection and denote a lack of defensiveness.

They whisper of an openness to ideas, feedback, and collaboration.

- **Nodding** at appropriate moments acknowledges understanding and agreement, reinforcing the speaker's points and showing alignment with their perspective.

Recovery from Trust Breaches

When trust is fractured, the path to restoration is paved with humility, patience, and concerted effort. Here are steps to rebuild trust once it's been compromised:

- **Immediate Acknowledgment**: Recognize the breach quickly. This initial step is crucial in demonstrating awareness of the impact of one's actions.

- **Genuine Apology**: Offer an apology that reflects a deep understanding of how the breach affected the other person. It's not merely about saying "I'm sorry" but about conveying a heartfelt regret for the harm caused.

- **Transparent Communication**: Engage in open and honest dialogue about the breach. Discuss what went wrong and why, and share thoughts and feelings frankly. This level of transparency is key to rebuilding trust.

- **Consistent Actions Over Words**: Follow through on promises and commitments. Repeated, reliable behavior over time is the strongest testament to one's dedication to mending the relationship.

Case Studies on Trust Building

Real-life examples offer valuable insights into the dynamics of trust-building. Here are narratives from both personal and professional realms that highlight successful trust restoration efforts:

- **A Business Partnership Tested**: Two entrepreneurs faced a crossroads when a significant financial loss threatened their venture. The mishap, caused by one partner's oversight, strained their relationship. However, through acknowledging the mistake, engaging in transparent communication about their fears and hopes for the business, and committing to specific steps to avoid future errors, they managed to salvage their partnership. Their business not only recovered but also flourished, buoyed by a renewed sense of trust and collaboration.

- **Friendship on the Brink**: A long-standing friendship was nearly undone by a misunderstanding exacerbated by third-party gossip. The accused friend took the initiative to reach out, seeking a face-to-face meeting to clear the air. Through honest conversation, both expressing their hurt and listening to the other's perspective, they were able to see past the rumors. They committed to direct communication in the future, reinforcing their bond through a mutual pledge to transparency and openness.

These stories underscore the resilience of trust when nurtured with honesty, openness, and a commitment to growth and understanding. They remind us that trust, once broken, can be rebuilt, but the process requires time, patience, and a willingness to engage in the hard work of genuine communication and consistent action.

5.2 The Ethics of Reading People: Responsible Use of Knowledge

Navigating the waters of human interaction with the skill to read people and detect deception brings with it a significant ethical responsibility. This ability, potent in its capacity to reveal unspoken truths, demands careful consideration of its implications and applications. As we refine these skills, we must also cultivate an ethical compass to guide us, ensuring that our endeavors respect the dignity and privacy of those we seek to understand.

Ethical Considerations

The ethical landscape surrounding the reading of people is complex, woven with questions of morality, privacy, and consent. When we peer into the realm of unspoken cues and hidden emotions, we tread on personal territory. The information gained, while valuable, must be approached with a sense of duty to use it wisely and compassionately. This responsibility extends to recognizing the potential impact of our interpretations and actions on relationships, reputations, and trust.

- **Privacy Respect**: At the core of ethical reading is respect for an individual's privacy. The ability to pick up on subtle cues should not serve as an invitation to pry into personal affairs without clear permission.

- **Informed Consent**: In situations where a deeper analysis is warranted, such as in professional settings or when helping a friend, obtaining informed consent becomes crucial. This process involves making sure individuals understand why you're reading them and how the insights gained will be used.

- **Avoiding Harm**: The principle of non-maleficence, or not causing harm, is paramount. The knowledge we acquire should not be used to manipulate, embarrass, or disadvantage others.

Boundaries of Application

Knowing when and where to apply the skills of reading people is as important as the skills themselves. Clear boundaries help safeguard against misuse and ensure our efforts contribute positively to our interactions.

- **Professional vs. Personal**: Distinguish between professional scenarios where reading people is part of your role, and personal situations where it might be seen as intrusive or unwelcome.

- **Sensitivity to Context**: Some contexts, such as grief or trauma, require heightened sensitivity. In these cases, the primary aim should be to offer support and understanding, rather than to analyze or uncover deceit.

- **Scope of Interpretation**: Be mindful of the limits of your ability to read people. Avoid overstepping by making broad judgments based on limited observations.

The Power of Empathy

Empathy not only enriches our connections with others but also serves as a moral guide in the responsible use of our skills. It reminds us to consider the feelings and perspectives of those we read, fostering an approach grounded in compassion and understanding.

- **Empathetic Listening**: More than just observing non-verbal cues, empathetic listening involves truly hearing and valuing the experiences and emotions of others. This form of engagement builds trust and opens avenues for genuine communication.

- **Compassionate Response**: Armed with insights into another's emotional state, the empathetic response involves offering support, validation, and kindness, rather than judgment or unsolicited advice.

- **Understanding vs. Exploitation**: Empathy steers us toward using our knowledge to understand and connect with others, rather than for personal gain or to exploit vulnerabilities.

Developing an Ethical Framework

As we advance our ability to read people, developing a personal ethical framework provides a foundation for integrity and respect in our interactions. This framework should include:

- **Reflective Practice**: Regular reflection on your motivations and the outcomes of your actions helps maintain an ethical stance. Consider keeping a journal to explore the ethical dimensions of your practice and to document situations where ethical dilemmas arise.

- **Seeking Guidance**: Engage with mentors, colleagues, or professionals who can offer advice and perspective on ethical issues related to reading people. This community can provide support and accountability as you navigate complex situations.

- **Continuous Learning**: Stay informed about the ethical considerations in your field, especially if your profession involves reading people as a significant component. Workshops, literature, and discussions on ethics contribute to an evolving understanding of how to apply your skills responsibly.

- **Commitment to Principles**: Define a set of core principles, such as respect for autonomy, commitment to honesty, and dedication to compassion, that guide your interactions. These principles serve as a compass, directing your actions and decisions.

In cultivating the skills to read people, we embark on a path that holds the potential for profound insights into human behavior and emotions. Yet, with this power comes the responsibility to navigate the ethical dimensions with care, ensuring our actions uphold the values of respect, consent, and empathy. As we develop an ethical framework to guide our practice, we not only protect the dignity of those we seek to understand but also enrich our own moral compass, leading to more meaningful and conscientious interactions in every facet of our lives.

5.3 Techniques for Law Enforcement: Reading Suspects Ethically

In the realm of law enforcement, the ability to read suspects offers a pivotal tool in the quest for truth. However, wielding this tool demands a careful balance between effective investigation and the preservation of individual rights. This section explores the ethical landscape of interrogation, the importance of training in non-verbal cues, and real-world dilemmas that highlight the nuanced dance between duty and decency.

Ethical Interrogation Techniques

Interrogation, a cornerstone of law enforcement's investigative process, must be conducted within an ethical framework that respects both the suspect's rights and the pursuit of justice. Traditional methods, while effective, sometimes toe the line of coercion, raising ethical red flags. Modern approaches emphasize a rapport-based technique, focusing on building a connection with the suspect to encourage voluntary sharing of information. This method not only upholds ethical standards but also reduces the risk of false confessions, ensuring that the information gathered is both reliable and legally sound.

- **Active Listening**: Demonstrating genuine interest in the suspect's story encourages openness, providing investigators with more nuanced insights.

- **Open-ended Questions**: These allow the suspect to narrate their account without leading them, reducing the risk of inadvertently planting information.

- **Transparency**: Clearly explaining the process and what's at stake helps to alleviate fear and confusion, fostering a more cooperative environment.

Balancing Rights and Responsibilities

The delicate act of balancing the rights of individuals against the responsibilities of law enforcement is a constant challenge. Officers must navigate this terrain with a keen awareness of the legal and moral implications of their actions. Training programs emphasize the importance of understanding constitutional rights, such as the right to remain silent and the right against self-incrimination, ensuring that officers respect these boundaries during interrogations. Moreover, adopting a mindset that seeks information rather than merely confirming pre-existing suspicions contributes to a more ethical approach.

- **Respect for Individual Dignity**: Treating suspects with dignity regardless of the accusations against them underpins ethical law enforcement practices.

- **Avoidance of Coercion**: Steering clear of physical or psychological pressure ensures that any confession or information obtained is both ethical and admissible in court.

- **Documentation**: Meticulously recording interrogations provides transparency and accountability, protecting both the suspect's rights and the integrity of the investigation.

Training in Non-Verbal Cues

Specialized training programs equip law enforcement officers with the skills to interpret non-verbal cues, a critical component in assessing a suspect's credibility and emotional state. These programs cover a broad spectrum of behaviors, from facial expressions and body language to voice pitch and hesitation patterns. Officers learn to discern the subtle signs of stress, deception, and compliance, enabling them to navigate interrogations with greater insight and sensitivity.

- **Facial Expression Analysis**: Training focuses on recognizing microexpressions — brief, involuntary facial expressions that reveal true emotions.

- **Body Language Interpretation**: Learning to read body language, such as posture, movement, and the use of space, provides clues to a suspect's mindset and truthfulness.

- **Vocal Analysis**: Understanding changes in speech patterns, tone, and rate can offer additional insights into a suspect's emotional state and credibility.

Case Studies of Ethical Dilemmas

Real-life scenarios underscore the ethical complexities faced by law enforcement when reading suspects. These case studies illuminate the challenges and strategies employed to navigate ethical dilemmas successfully.

- **A High-Profile Case**: An officer interrogating a suspect in a high-profile theft case noticed inconsistencies in the suspect's story. Rather than confront these discrepancies aggressively, the officer used rapport-based techniques, asking open-ended questions that allowed the suspect to reveal more information voluntarily. This approach not only respected the suspect's rights but also led to a breakthrough in the case.

- **A Misunderstanding Escalated**: In another instance, a misunderstanding between officers about a suspect's non-verbal cues led to a wrongful accusation. The suspect's nervous behavior, a result of anxiety rather than guilt, was misinterpreted as deceptive. This case highlighted the need for comprehensive training in reading non-verbal cues and the importance of considering the suspect's baseline behavior and external stress factors.

These case studies demonstrate the importance of ethical considerations in law enforcement's ability to read suspects. They emphasize the need for ongoing training, a commitment to respecting individual rights, and an understanding of the psychological underpinnings of behavior. Through these lenses, law enforcement can navigate the thin line between effective investigation and ethical practice, ensuring that justice is served with integrity and respect for human dignity.

5.4 Advanced Negotiation Tactics: Reading the Room and Influencing Outcomes

Navigating the nuanced waters of negotiation requires more than just verbal prowess and a solid grasp of the facts. It demands a deep understanding of human psychology and the ability to read and influence others through both spoken and unspoken language. In high-stakes negotiation settings, where the balance of power can shift with a single word or gesture, mastering these skills can make the difference between a favorable outcome and a missed opportunity.

Psychological Strategies in Negotiation

At the heart of effective negotiation lies the strategic use of psychological insights to understand and influence the behavior of others. Techniques such as framing, anchoring, and the use of strategic silence play pivotal roles.

- **Framing**: This involves presenting information in a way that emphasizes the benefits or minimizes the drawbacks from the perspective of the other party. It's about shaping how the proposal is viewed, making it more appealing.

- **Anchoring**: The first number put on the table sets the 'anchor' for the negotiation. Even if it's outrageously high or low, it establishes a psychological benchmark for the discussion.

- **Strategic Silence**: Sometimes, saying nothing is the most powerful statement. Silence after making an offer or presenting a point can compel the other party to fill the void, often revealing more than they intended or agreeing to terms more favorable to you.

Understanding and applying these strategies requires keen observation and adaptability, as the effectiveness of each can vary dramatically depending on the context and the individuals involved.

Non-Verbal Communication in Negotiation

The silent signals we send and receive — our body language — can significantly impact negotiations. Being adept at reading these cues and consciously controlling your own can provide a critical advantage.

- **Posture and Presence**: A confident stance and calm demeanor can convey authority and assurance, often persuading the other party of your strong position without a word being spoken.

- **Facial Expressions**: A genuine smile can disarm and foster a sense of camaraderie, while maintaining a neutral expression can mask your true feelings about the discussion or offer on the table.

- **Gestural Feedback**: Subtle nods can encourage the speaker to continue, showing engagement without interrupting, while folded arms might suggest skepticism or defensiveness, signaling a need to reassess your approach.

Mastering the art of non-verbal communication allows you to send and interpret signals that transcend words, providing insights into the emotions and intentions that underlie the spoken dialogue.

Building Rapport in Negotiation Settings

Establishing a connection with the other party is crucial for successful negotiation. Rapport creates a foundation of trust and respect that can facilitate open dialogue, making it easier to find common ground and reach mutually beneficial agreements.

- **Common Ground**: Begin by identifying shared interests or goals. Highlighting these early on can set a positive tone for the discussion.

- **Active Listening**: Show genuine interest in understanding the other party's needs and concerns. This not only provides valuable information but also demonstrates respect, which can soften adversarial stances.

- **Adaptability**: Be prepared to adjust your communication style to better align with the other party. Mirroring their tone and language can foster a sense of similarity and comfort.

Fostering rapport doesn't mean avoiding tough conversations but rather establishing a framework within which those conversations can occur more productively.

Real-World Negotiation Scenarios

Illustrating these concepts are stories from the negotiation front lines, where reading the room and employing advanced tactics led to outcomes that exceeded expectations.

In one notable instance, a mediator was brought into a long-standing dispute between two corporate divisions. By employing strategic silence at key moments, the mediator encouraged the parties to openly discuss their grievances, many of which stemmed from miscommunications and false assumptions. This approach, combined with anchoring the discussions around a shared goal of organizational success, led to a resolution that had seemed impossible.

Another example involves a startup founder negotiating with potential investors. Recognizing the importance of non-verbal cues, the founder maintained open body language and matched the investors' conversational tone, fostering an atmosphere of collaboration. By framing the investment opportunity in terms of its potential for societal impact — a value important to the investors — the founder secured the funding needed, with terms more favorable than initially expected.

These scenarios underscore the power of psychological strategies, non-verbal communication, and rapport-building in negotiation. They highlight not just the complexity of human interaction but also the potential for achieving remarkable outcomes when we approach these interactions with insight, empathy, and strategic acumen.

As we wrap up this exploration into the dynamics of negotiation, we're reminded of the intricate dance of human interaction. The ability to read the room, understand the underlying currents of emotion and thought, and strategically influence the outcome is a skill that, while complex, can be developed with practice and intention. These advanced tactics not only enrich our toolkit for negotiation but also deepen our understanding of the subtleties of communication, paving the way for more meaningful and effective engagements in all areas of our lives.

Looking ahead, the journey through the labyrinth of human behavior and interaction continues to unfold, offering endless opportunities for discovery and growth.

CHAPTER 6

Enhancing Your Observational Tapestry

In a bustling café on a crisp morning, the steam from your coffee rises and mingles with the murmur of conversations, the clinking of cups. You're not just a spectator in this scene; you're a participant in a living, breathing tapestry of human interaction. Observing people isn't about uncovering secrets or making judgments. It's about understanding the rich complexity of human behavior and appreciating the silent stories told through gestures, expressions, and the subtle dance of interaction. This chapter guides you through honing your observational skills, turning everyday moments into opportunities for insight and connection.

Routine Observations

The world around us is a classroom, and daily life offers a curriculum rich in lessons on human behavior. Start by setting a simple goal: choose one public place you frequent—be it a café, a park, or public transport—and dedicate ten minutes to observation. Focus on non-verbal cues: a couple leaning in close sharing a secret, a hurried commuter's quickened pace, or the expansive posture of someone engrossed in a book. These moments are like brush strokes in the broader picture of human emotion and interaction.

- **Morning Commute**: Notice the array of expressions and postures. Who is lost in thought, and who is visibly stressed? What does that say about their current state or where they're headed?

- **Lunch Break at the Park**: Witness the dynamics of groups versus individuals. How do people occupy space when alone versus with others? What does this reveal about comfort levels and social relationships?

Journaling Insights

Keeping a journal of your observations not only tracks progress but also deepens your understanding. After each observation session, jot down notable behaviors and your interpretations. Did someone's furrowed brow while checking their phone suggest worry, or were they simply squinting in the sunlight? Over time, patterns emerge, offering insights into the common threads of human behavior and your evolving perceptions.

- **Daily Prompts**: At the end of each day, reflect on one interaction that stood out. Describe the setting, the players, and the non-verbal cues observed. What story do these cues tell?

- **Weekly Reflections**: Set aside time each week to review your entries. Note any changes in your observational skills or new insights gained. How has this practice affected your interactions and perceptions?

Comparative Analysis

Enhance your accuracy in reading people by comparing observed behaviors with known baseline behaviors. This comparison requires familiarity, so start with friends or family members, noting how they express emotions like joy, frustration, or surprise. When you observe similar emotions in strangers, compare the behaviors. Is the stranger's smile as genuine as your friend's ear-to-ear grin, or does it not quite reach their eyes?

- **Family Gatherings**: Use these as opportunities to observe and note baseline behaviors in a familiar setting.

- **Public Spaces**: Observe strangers displaying similar emotions. How do their expressions and gestures compare to your baseline observations?

Feedback Loop

Seeking feedback on your observations is crucial for growth. Share your interpretations with a trusted friend or family member, especially if they were present during the observation. Did they perceive the situation similarly, or did they pick up on cues you missed? This feedback sharpens your skills, offering new perspectives and correcting any biases or misinterpretations.

- **Discussion with Peers**: After an outing with friends, discuss your observations. Was there consensus on the non-verbal cues noticed?

- **Mentor Insights**: If you have a mentor experienced in reading people, discuss your journal entries. Their expertise can provide valuable guidance and correction.

This chapter not only equips you with the tools to enhance your observational skills but also invites you to weave these practices into the fabric of your daily life. By turning routine observations into a habit, journaling insights to reflect and grow, comparing behaviors to understand the nuance of human emotion, and engaging in a feedback loop to refine your interpretations, you enrich your tapestry of human understanding. These practices illuminate the silent stories around us, fostering a deeper connection to the world and the people who animate it.

6.1 Emotional Intelligence Workouts: Enhancing Your EQ Through Practice

The fabric of our interactions is woven with threads of emotion. Recognizing, understanding, and managing these threads can transform the way we connect with the world. Emotional Intelligence (EQ) is not a static trait; it's a set of skills that can be developed with intention and practice. This section introduces exercises designed to fine-tune your EQ, turning everyday encounters into a gymnasium for emotional growth.

Emotion Identification

The first step towards emotional intelligence is recognizing emotions as they arise, both in ourselves and others. This recognition is the foundation upon which empathy and emotional management are built.

- **Real-time Emotion Tracking**: Throughout your day, pause at random intervals to assess your emotional state. Are you feeling anxious, excited, or perhaps a bit melancholy? Note these emotions down, along with what you think might be causing them. This practice cultivates self-awareness, a key component of EQ.

- **Emotion Spotting in Others**: While interacting with others, try to identify their emotions based on cues like tone of voice, facial expressions, and body language. After your conversation, verify your observations by asking them how they were feeling. This not only improves your ability to read others but also deepens your connection with them.

Perspective-Taking

Empathy grows from the soil of understanding. By stepping into another's shoes, we gain insights into their feelings and viewpoints, nurturing a deeper connection.

- **The 'Why' Game**: Choose a person you interact with regularly and spend a day considering the reasons behind their actions and emotions. For every behavior or emotion you observe, ask yourself "Why might they feel or act this way?" This helps in developing a habit of looking beyond the surface, fostering empathy and understanding.

- **Role Reversal**: Pair up with a friend or family member and share a recent experience or challenge. Then, swap roles: you'll argue their perspective, and they'll argue yours. This exercise not only broadens your viewpoint but also highlights the complexity of emotions and motivations.

Mindfulness Practices

Mindfulness is the anchor that keeps us grounded in the tumultuous sea of emotions. By cultivating mindfulness, we enhance our ability to remain present and composed, regardless of the emotional storms we might face.

- **Breath Focused Meditation**: Begin or end your day with a five-minute meditation, focusing solely on your breath. Each time your mind wanders to thoughts or worries, gently bring your focus back to your breath. This practice enhances your ability to stay centered amidst emotional upheaval.

- **Emotional Surfing**: When you find yourself caught in a wave of strong emotion, rather than reacting impulsively, pause and observe the emotion. Imagine it as a wave: it rises, crests, and eventually falls. This visualization helps in regulating emotions, promoting a balanced response rather than a reactive one.

Role-Playing Scenarios

Role-playing places you in controlled, yet emotionally charged scenarios, offering a safe space to explore and manage diverse emotional landscapes.

- **Conflict Resolution**: With a partner, simulate a conflict scenario where both parties have opposing viewpoints. Take turns expressing your side, focusing on maintaining empathy and composure. Afterward, discuss the emotions each of you experienced and explore alternative, emotionally intelligent responses.

- **Emotional Support Role-Play**: One partner shares a problem they're facing, while the other practices offering support, focusing on empathetic listening and emotional validation. Swap roles and then discuss the experience, paying particular attention to the emotions stirred by offering and receiving support.

These exercises are your tools for sculpting a more emotionally intelligent self. Like any skill, mastery comes with consistent practice. By integrating these workouts into your daily routine, you weave emotional intelligence into the fabric of your being, enriching your interactions and deepening your connections.

6.2 Role-Playing Scenarios: Practicing Your Skills in Safe Environments

Exploring the dynamics of human interaction through role-playing exercises provides a unique canvas where theoretical knowledge meets practical application. This method allows for a deeper immersion into the multifaceted world of communication, granting us the freedom to experiment, observe, and refine our approach in understanding and connecting with others.

Structured Role-Play

Creating structured role-playing scenarios is akin to setting the stage for a play where each participant performs a part, yet the script is unwritten, and the outcome undefined. This process involves:

- **Choosing Roles**: Participants select roles that could range from everyday situations, like a disagreement with a friend, to more complex interactions, such as a job interview or a sensitive conversation with a loved one.

- **Setting the Scene**: Define the context and objectives for each scenario. What is the background of this interaction? What does each participant hope to achieve?

- **Guided Performance**: As the scenario unfolds, encourage participants to fully embody their roles, paying close attention to their use of verbal and non-verbal communication.

This method not only enhances one's ability to read cues and adapt responses but also fosters a deeper empathy by placing oneself in another's shoes.

Feedback Mechanisms

The gold that is gleaned from these role-playing exercises often lies in the feedback shared post-performance. This step is where growth is catalyzed, transforming experience into insight. Effective feedback mechanisms include:

- **Pause and Reflect**: Immediately after the role-play, allow a moment for participants to reflect on their experience. What emotions were stirred? What challenges emerged?

- **Constructive Criticism**: Feedback should strike a balance between highlighting strengths and identifying areas for improvement. It's vital that this exchange is rooted in respect and the desire to aid growth, not diminish confidence.

- **Group Discussion**: Involve all participants in the feedback process. Often, observers can offer valuable perspectives that those in the role-play might have missed.

This collaborative review of the role-play enriches the learning experience, providing multiple lenses through which to view the interaction.

Diverse Scenarios

To truly harness the potential of role-playing exercises, it's crucial to traverse a broad spectrum of scenarios. This diversity not only broadens the application of one's skills but also prepares one for the unpredictable nature of human interactions. Scenarios to consider might include:

- **Professional**: Negotiating a contract, resolving workplace conflict, or leading a team meeting. These situations hone one's ability to navigate the professional realm with tact and empathy.

- **Social**: Planning an event with friends, addressing a misunderstanding, or engaging in small talk at a social gathering. These interactions help sharpen one's skills in reading social cues and fostering positive relationships.

- **Intimate**: Discussing relationship issues, expressing needs or concerns, or supporting a partner through a difficult time. These deeply personal interactions demand a high level of emotional intelligence and sensitivity.

By stepping into varied roles across different contexts, participants gain a richer, more nuanced understanding of the myriad ways we communicate and connect.

Reflection and Adjustment

After the curtain falls on each role-playing exercise, reflection paves the way for adjustment and growth. This introspective process involves:

- **Self-Assessment**: Participants review their performance, assessing how effectively they communicated, read cues, and adapted their behavior. Did they achieve their objectives? How did their actions impact the interaction?

- **Identifying Patterns**: Look for recurring themes in feedback and self-assessment. Are there specific areas where improvement is consistently suggested? Recognizing patterns helps focus future efforts on areas most in need of development.

- **Setting Intentions for Growth**: Based on these reflections, participants set targeted goals for enhancing their skills. This might involve practicing specific aspects of non-verbal communication, developing a greater awareness of one's emotional responses, or seeking out additional resources for learning.

Through this cycle of action, reflection, and adjustment, role-playing exercises evolve from simple simulations to powerful tools for personal and interpersonal development. They offer a safe space to explore the complexities of human interaction, experiment with different strategies, and refine one's ability to navigate the rich tapestry of communication that binds us all.

6.3 The Power of Feedback: Learning Through Reflection

Navigating the intricate dance of human interactions, the feedback we receive and give ourselves is akin to a mirror, providing a reflection that guides our growth in reading others. This segment explores the multifaceted approach to engaging with feedback, a vital component in the tapestry of understanding human behavior.

Seeking Constructive Criticism

Inviting criticism, especially about something as personal as our ability to understand others, requires a blend of humility and courage. It's an art in itself, knowing whom to ask, how to ask, and most importantly, how to process the insights offered. Here's a roadmap to navigate this terrain:

- **Selecting the Right Sources**: Look for individuals whose judgment you trust and who have demonstrated a keen understanding of human behavior themselves. These could be mentors, colleagues, or friends known for their insightful observations.

- **Framing Your Request**: Be specific about what you're seeking feedback on. Is it your interpretation of non-verbal cues during a particular interaction, or how well you managed to maintain empathy in a challenging conversation? Clarity helps the reviewer provide focused, actionable insights.

- **Creating a Safe Space**: Ensure the conversation takes place in a setting where both you and the reviewer feel comfortable speaking openly. A relaxed atmosphere can foster a more honest exchange.

- **Embracing Vulnerability**: Approach the feedback with an open mind. Remember, the goal is improvement, not validation.

Self-Assessment

The journey towards mastering the art of reading people begins with an inward look. Self-assessment is a tool that sharpens our self-awareness, allowing us to understand our baseline capabilities and areas ripe for development. Here are strategies to make self-assessment a regular part of your growth process:

- **Regular Reflection**: After significant interactions or at the end of each day, take a moment to reflect on your observations and interactions. Did you notice any cues you might have missed before? How accurate were your interpretations?

- **Emotion Journaling**: Keep a log of your emotional responses during different interactions. Over time, patterns will emerge, highlighting biases or triggers that may color your interpretation of others.

- **Recording and Reviewing**: If possible, record practice conversations (with consent) and review them. Pay attention not just to what was said, but how it was conveyed. This can reveal discrepancies between your perception in the moment and the reality of the interaction.

Integrating Feedback

Receiving feedback is just the first step; integrating it into practice is where the real growth happens. This process involves translating insights into actionable steps. Here's how to make feedback a powerful catalyst for improvement:

- **Break It Down**: Deconstruct the feedback into specific, manageable elements. If the feedback is "You need to improve your empathy," identify concrete actions, like "practice active listening" or "observe emotional responses without judgment."

- **Set Specific Goals**: For each element, set clear, achievable goals. If active listening is the target, a goal might be to summarize what the other person has said before offering your perspective, in at least three conversations each day.

- **Track Progress**: Keep a record of your efforts towards these goals. This not only provides motivation but also helps you see the tangible outcomes of integrating the feedback.

- **Iterate**: Based on your progress, adjust your goals and strategies. Feedback integration is not a one-time task but an ongoing process.

Continuous Learning Cycle

At its core, the pursuit of understanding others is a journey without end, a continuous cycle of observation, practice, feedback, and adjustment. Embracing this cycle means accepting that there will always be more to learn, and each step taken is a step towards greater insight. Here's what this cycle entails:

- **Observation**: Always be on the lookout for new patterns, behaviors, and interactions to analyze. Life offers an endless stream of lessons on human behavior.

- **Practice**: Use every interaction as an opportunity to apply what you've learned, whether it's recognizing microexpressions, maintaining empathy, or interpreting body language.

- **Feedback**: Seek and provide feedback regularly. This could be through formal sessions with a mentor or informal discussions with peers.

- **Adjustment**: Use the insights gained from feedback and self-assessment to refine your approach and techniques. This might mean focusing on new areas for observation or experimenting with different methods of engagement.

By weaving these elements into the fabric of your daily life, you transform the process of learning to read people from a series of discrete actions into a rich, ongoing journey of discovery. Each interaction, each piece of feedback, and each moment of reflection adds another thread to the intricate tapestry of human understanding you're continuously crafting.

6.4 Creating Your Personal Action Plan for Continuous Improvement

In the realm of understanding and connecting with others, setting a course for continual growth is akin to charting a map through unexplored territories. Each step taken, each skill honed, brings us closer to a deeper comprehension of the intricate dance of human interaction. This section unwraps the process of crafting a personal action plan tailored to your unique path towards enhancing your ability to read people.

Personalized Goals

Embarking on this path requires a clear vision of your destination. Begin by identifying what aspects of reading people you wish to improve. Is it deciphering the subtle cues of body language, or perhaps, deepening your empathetic listening? With these focal points in mind, set goals that resonate with your personal strengths and the areas you're eager to develop. For example, if your aim is to better understand emotional cues:

- Set a goal to recognize and correctly interpret one new emotional cue per week.

- Commit to observing interactions in a specific setting, like meetings or family dinners, to practice and apply your growing knowledge.

Actionable Steps

With your goals in sight, breaking them into manageable steps ensures they're within reach. Each step should be actionable and defined by a clear timeline, transforming your aspirations into a roadmap of attainable milestones. Consider employing the SMART criteria — Specific, Measurable, Achievable, Relevant, Time-bound — to guide this process. If improving empathetic listening is a goal:

- Dedicate two conversations each day to practice active listening, focusing fully on the speaker without formulating a response until they've finished.

- After each conversation, take a moment to reflect on what you've learned about the speaker's emotional state or needs.

Resource Allocation

The journey towards mastery is supported by a wealth of resources waiting to be tapped. Identify books, online courses, or workshops that align with your goals. Seek out mentors or peers who share your interest in understanding human behavior and can offer guidance or join you in practice sessions. Allocate time each week to engage with these resources, treating them as investments in your personal growth. Resources might include:

- A well-reviewed book on body language, scheduled for reading over the next month.

- A weekly meeting with a mentor or peer to discuss observations and experiences, providing mutual support and insight.

Regular Review

Setting a regular cadence for reviewing your progress keeps you aligned with your goals and responsive to the insights gained along the way. This can be a monthly or quarterly review session where you assess what's working, what challenges you've faced, and how your goals may have shifted based on your experiences. Celebrate the milestones reached, no matter how small, and adjust your plan as needed to reflect your evolving understanding and aspirations. This review process might involve:

- Reflecting on the emotional cues you've successfully identified and understood, noting any patterns or surprises in your observations.

- Revisiting your goals and steps to ensure they still align with your aspirations, making adjustments based on your progress and any new areas of interest that have emerged.

As we wrap up this exploration into creating a personalized action plan for continuous improvement, we are reminded of the power inherent in setting a deliberate course towards understanding the nuances of human interaction. By establishing clear goals, breaking them into actionable steps, tapping into a wealth of resources, and regularly reviewing progress, we set the stage for meaningful growth and deeper connections. This process, while personal and unique to each individual, contributes to a collective enrichment of our interactions and relationships, enhancing the fabric of our shared humanity.

With these strategies in hand, we move forward, equipped to navigate the complexities of human behavior with greater insight and empathy, ready to face the challenges and opportunities that lie ahead in our continuous quest for understanding.

CHAPTER 7

Navigating the Fog: Embracing the Complexities of Human Behavior

Imagine you're standing at the edge of a misty forest. The path ahead is not clear, and the usual markers you rely on are obscured by the fog. Yet, there's a certain allure in the unknown, a promise of discovery despite the uncertainty. This is much like the process of reading people. Despite our best efforts, individuals often defy easy categorization, their motives and emotions shrouded in complexity. This chapter delves into embracing the ambiguity inherent in human behavior, offering strategies to navigate these uncertainties with confidence and curiosity.

Accepting Uncertainty

Reading people is far from a clear-cut science. Just as every person is a unique amalgamation of experiences, thoughts, and emotions, the signals they emit can be equally complex and contradictory. Accepting that ambiguity is a natural part of human interaction is the first step towards becoming more adept at reading people. It's about learning to be comfortable with the questions as much as the answers, understanding that sometimes, the full picture may not immediately be clear—or may never fully reveal itself.

Strategies for dealing with this uncertainty include:

- **Embrace a Learner's Mindset**: Approach each interaction with the openness and curiosity of a lifelong learner. Acknowledge that there's always something new to discover about human behavior.

- **Practice Patience**: Give yourself time to observe and absorb the nuances of an interaction. Rushing to conclusions can often lead to misunderstandings.

Strategies for Uncertainty

When faced with mixed signals or incomplete information, having a set of strategies can help you make more informed interpretations. Consider the following:

- **Gather More Data**: Before drawing conclusions, look for additional cues. This might mean observing the person in different contexts or seeking input from others who know them well.

- **Ask Open-Ended Questions**: Encourage the person to share more about their thoughts and feelings. This can provide clarity and offer new insights into their behavior.

- **Compare Against Known Behaviors**: If you're familiar with the person, compare their current behavior with their typical behavior patterns. Significant deviations can be telling.

Comfort with Incompleteness

Not every puzzle will be solved, and not every question will have an answer. Finding comfort in the incomplete nature of our understanding of others is crucial. This doesn't mean giving up on trying to understand but recognizing the limits of our perception. It's about making peace with the idea that some aspects of human behavior may remain a mystery, and that's okay. This acceptance can free us from the frustration of unmet expectations and allow us to focus on what we can learn and understand.

- **Reflect on Past Experiences**: Think back on times when your initial read on someone was incomplete or incorrect. Reflect on how your understanding evolved over time.

- **Journaling**: Keeping a journal about your experiences trying to read people can help you track patterns in your interpretations and how they've changed with added information.

Flexibility in Interpretations

Holding your interpretations lightly allows you to be open to new information that can alter your understanding of someone's behavior. This flexibility is key in effectively reading people, as it enables you to update your perceptions as you gather more insights.

- **Stay Open to New Information**: Even if you feel confident in your read on someone, be willing to adjust your understanding as new information comes to light.

- **Practice Scenario Planning**: Consider multiple possible explanations for a behavior. This exercise can help you avoid becoming too attached to a single interpretation and remain open to various possibilities.

In our daily interactions, we often find ourselves in situations where the behavior of others doesn't fit neatly into our existing frameworks of understanding. For instance, a friend might react to news with an unexpected emotion, or a colleague's body language might contradict their words during a meeting. In these moments, it's tempting to jump to conclusions based on our initial read. However, by adopting a learner's mindset, practicing patience, and employing the strategies outlined above, we can navigate these uncertainties more effectively.

- **In the Workplace**: When a colleague's behavior seems out of character, instead of drawing immediate conclusions, observe over time and ask open-ended questions to understand their perspective better.

- **In Personal Relationships**: If a friend's reaction to news surprises you, consider what you know about their past experiences that might influence their response. Engage in a conversation that allows them to express their feelings more fully.

By embracing the complexities and ambiguities of human behavior, we not only become better at reading others but also enrich our interactions with a deeper sense of empathy and understanding. This approach doesn't simplify the intricate nature of human emotions and motives; instead, it acknowledges the beauty and richness in the fog, inviting us to step into the unknown with curiosity and openness.

7.1 Overcoming Personal Biases: The Journey Towards Objectivity

In the intricate tapestry of human interaction, our perceptions are often colored by a myriad of personal biases. These biases, while sometimes subtle, can significantly skew our understanding of others, leading to misinterpretations and misunderstandings. The process of identifying and mitigating these biases is not only about refining our ability to read people more accurately but also about fostering deeper connections through a more empathetic lens.

Identifying Biases

The first step in this process is recognizing the biases that lurk in the corners of our perceptions. These can range from the relatively straightforward, such as the tendency to favor those who share our interests, to the more insidious, like unconscious stereotypes that influence how we view people from different backgrounds. To unearth these biases, we must:

- Reflect on Past Interactions: Review your memories of past interactions, paying close attention to instances where your initial impressions were later proven incorrect. What assumptions did you make, and why?

- Seek Feedback: Sometimes, biases are more visible to those around us than they are to ourselves. Engaging in honest conversations with trusted individuals about how you perceive others can unveil biases you weren't aware of.

- Exposure to Diversity: Exposing yourself to a wide range of perspectives and cultures can illuminate biases born from a lack of understanding or exposure.

Mitigating Biases

Once identified, the challenge lies in mitigating the influence of these biases on our perceptions. This requires active effort and strategies, including:

- Conscious Counteracting: When you catch yourself making assumptions based on a bias, consciously challenge these thoughts. Ask yourself, "Would I feel the same if the person were from a different background or held different beliefs?"

- Diversify Your Circle: Actively seek out and engage with people who come from different walks of life. This not only broadens your perspective but also helps break down stereotypes and assumptions.

- Education and Awareness: Commit to learning about the histories, cultures, and experiences of others. Understanding the context of people's lives can significantly reduce the impact of biases.

Empathy as a Tool

Empathy is a powerful ally in the quest to see beyond our biases. By striving to understand the emotions, thoughts, and experiences of others from their point of view, we can transcend the limitations of our own perspectives. To harness empathy effectively:

- Practice Active Listening: Listen to understand, not to respond. By focusing fully on the other person's words and emotions, you can gain insights that go beyond surface-level interpretations.

- Emotionally Imagine Yourself in Their Place: When interacting with someone, take a moment to imagine what it might be like to be in their situation. This mental exercise can shift your perspective and reduce the impact of biases.

- Validate Their Experiences: Acknowledging and validating someone's feelings or experiences, even if they differ vastly from your own, fosters a deeper connection and understanding.

Continuous Vigilance

The work of overcoming personal biases is ongoing. As our experiences shape and reshape our perceptions, new biases can emerge, requiring constant vigilance and self-reflection. To maintain this vigilance:

- Regular Check-ins With Yourself: Set aside time regularly to reflect on your interactions and perceptions. Have you noticed any patterns or biases influencing your behavior?

- Keep Learning: The more we learn about the world and the diverse tapestry of people in it, the more equipped we are to recognize and address our biases.

- Foster an Environment of Openness: Encourage open dialogue about biases and perceptions in your social and professional circles. This can lead to collective growth and understanding.

In every interaction, there lies an opportunity to peel back the layers of our biases and uncover the rich complexities of those around us. Whether it's in the subtle shift of perspective that comes from a heartfelt conversation or the broadening of understanding through new experiences, each step taken towards objectivity and empathy enriches our connections with others. It's a path that demands patience, openness, and a commitment to growth, but the rewards—a deeper understanding of the kaleidoscope of human behavior and the forging of genuine connections—are immeasurably valuable.

7.2 Handling Difficult Conversations: Strategies for Sensitive Situations

Navigating through the terrain of sensitive discussions demands a careful blend of preparation, empathy, and strategic communication. These conversations, whether they're about addressing performance issues at work, discussing relationship concerns, or delving into deeply personal topics, can test the limits of our emotional and interpersonal skills. Yet, with the right approach, they can also lead to breakthroughs, deeper understanding, and strengthened connections.

Preparation for Difficult Conversations

Entering into a challenging dialogue without groundwork is akin to navigating a ship through stormy seas without a compass. A bit of foresight can make all the difference. Here's how to set the stage:

- **Outline Your Objectives**: Clarify what you hope to achieve from the conversation. Is it to find a solution, to express your feelings, or to understand the other person's perspective? Knowing your goal will guide the flow of conversation.

- **Anticipate Their Response**: Think through how the other person might react. This can help you prepare emotionally and strategize how to keep the conversation constructive.

- **Plan Your Non-Verbal Cues**: Non-verbal communication speaks volumes. Plan to maintain an open posture and use calming gestures to foster a safe space for dialogue.

Active Listening

The role of active listening in managing tough talks cannot be overstated. It involves fully concentrating on what is being said rather than passively 'hearing' the message of the speaker. Active listening can transform a potential conflict into a moment of connection.

- **Summarize and Reflect**: Periodically summarize what the other person has said to show you're understanding their point of view. Reflection shows you're not just hearing, but also processing the information.

- **Ask Clarifying Questions**: If something isn't clear, ask open-ended questions that encourage the speaker to elaborate. This demonstrates your interest in fully grasping their perspective.

- **Avoid Interrupting**: Let the other person express their thoughts without interruption. This conveys respect and patience, crucial in a sensitive discussion.

Non-Verbal Empathy

In moments of heightened emotions, what we don't say often speaks louder than our words. Non-verbal cues of empathy can bridge gaps where words fall short.

- **Maintain Eye Contact**: Eye contact conveys you're engaged and present. It's a simple yet powerful way to show you're fully with the person.

- **Nodding**: A nod can communicate that you're following along without interrupting the flow of their speech.

- **Mirroring**: Subtly mirroring the other person's body language can create a sense of harmony and rapport, making it easier to navigate tough topics.

De-escalation Techniques

When emotions run high, a conversation can quickly escalate into a confrontation. De-escalation techniques are vital tools in redirecting the energy towards a more constructive outcome.

- **Stay Calm**: Your calmness can be contagious. By maintaining a composed demeanor, you set the tone for the interaction.

- **Use "I" Statements**: Communicate your feelings and thoughts using "I" statements. This reduces the likelihood of the other person feeling attacked, which can escalate tensions.

- **Take a Break**: If the conversation becomes too charged, suggest a brief pause. A moment of separation can allow emotions to cool and provide time for reflection.

- **Acknowledge Their Feelings**: Recognizing the other person's emotions without judgment can validate their experience and reduce defensiveness. "I can see this is really upsetting for you" is a simple way to show understanding.

In practice, these strategies are not just theoretical exercises but real-life tools that require patience, practice, and a genuine desire to connect deeply with others. For example, consider a scenario where you need to discuss a sensitive family issue. Before the talk, you take time to reflect on your goals and anticipate potential reactions, preparing yourself to stay composed and empathetic. As the conversation unfolds, you focus intently on listening, using nods and brief verbal affirmations to show you're engaged. When the discussion heats up, you remind yourself to breathe, using "I" statements to express your feelings calmly and taking a short break when needed.

Such an approach doesn't guarantee an immediate resolution or an easy conversation. However, it does pave the way for more meaningful dialogue, mutual understanding, and, ultimately, stronger relationships. Whether you're navigating the complexities of workplace dynamics, the intricacies of personal relationships, or the delicate balance of family interactions, these strategies offer a compass to guide you through the potentially turbulent waters of difficult conversations.

7.3 Resilience in the Face of Misinterpretation: Learning from Mistakes

Misinterpretations, much like the occasional rain on a sunny day, are inevitable in the intricate dance of understanding and connecting with others. While it's natural to strive for precision in our perceptions, the reality is that human interactions are layered with complexity. Recognizing that misunderstandings are part of the fabric of social exchanges paves the way for a more forgiving and growth-oriented approach.

Accepting Misinterpretation

The initial step in navigating the waters of misinterpretation involves acknowledging its inevitability. This acknowledgment doesn't signify a resignation to fate but rather a realistic acceptance of the human condition. Every individual we encounter is a living mosaic of experiences, beliefs, and emotions, making absolute accuracy in reading them an ambitious goal. Embrace misinterpretations as checkpoints rather than roadblocks, markers that highlight our engagement and investment in the process of understanding others.

- Reflect on instances of misinterpretation with curiosity rather than criticism. Ask yourself, "What did this experience teach me about the other person and myself?"

- Share your experiences with peers. Discussing misunderstandings in a supportive environment can demystify them and reinforce their role in the learning process.

Learning from Errors

The true measure of our ability to read others isn't in avoiding mistakes but in how we respond to and learn from them. Each misinterpretation offers a wealth of insights, providing a mirror to our own biases, assumptions, and areas for growth. To transform errors into lessons, consider the following:

- Conduct a post-mortem analysis of the interaction. Was the misinterpretation a result of preconceived notions, a lack of information, or perhaps misreading non-verbal cues?

- Experiment with adjustments in your approach. If assuming less and inquiring more could have led to a different outcome, integrate this strategy into future interactions.

Building Resilience

Cultivating resilience in the face of setbacks and criticism is akin to strengthening our emotional immune system. It involves developing a buffer that allows us to withstand the impact of mistakes without diminishing our willingness to engage and learn. Building resilience can be approached through:

- Regular self-care practices. Ensure that your physical and emotional well-being are priorities, creating a strong foundation from which to handle challenges.

- Establishing a support network. Surround yourself with individuals who encourage your growth and provide constructive feedback.

- Celebrate progress, not just perfection. Recognize and reward yourself for the steps taken towards improving your understanding of others, no matter how small.

Fostering a Growth Mindset

At the core of resilience lies a growth mindset, the belief that our abilities to understand and connect with others are not fixed but can be developed through dedication and hard work. This perspective sees challenges and errors as opportunities for expansion, driving us to explore beyond the boundaries of our current understanding.

- Embrace challenges as opportunities. When faced with a particularly complex interaction or a significant misinterpretation, view it as a chance to develop new skills and insights.

- Value effort over innate talent. Recognize that the process of getting better at reading people is a gradual one, requiring persistent effort rather than a reliance on natural ability.

- Learn from the success of others. Look to individuals renowned for their interpersonal skills, not as unreachable ideals but as sources of inspiration and learning.

In the nuanced realm of human interaction, resilience and a growth mindset are our most valuable allies. They enable us to navigate the inevitable misinterpretations and setbacks with grace, viewing each as a stepping stone towards deeper understanding and connection. As we move forward, let us remember that the richness of human behavior, with all its intricacies and ambiguities, offers an endless landscape for exploration and growth. The journey of understanding others is not a linear path but a spiral, where each cycle of misinterpretation and learning brings us closer to the heart of what it means to truly connect.

7.4 Cultivating Patience and Persistence: The Long Road to Mastery

Developing the ability to read people accurately is a skill that demands time and dedication. As we refine our observational skills, set realistic goals, and learn from each interaction, we're building a foundation for deeper understanding and connection. Here, we'll explore how patience, persistence, and celebrating every bit of progress are key to becoming proficient in interpreting the complexities of human behavior.

Setting Realistic Goals

Begin by acknowledging that the path to proficiency is gradual and filled with learning opportunities at every turn. Recognizing the layers and subtleties involved in human communication, it's important to set achievable goals that reflect the complexity of this endeavor. These might include improving your understanding of body language in certain situations or becoming more attuned to the nuances of vocal tone over time. Remember, small, attainable goals pave the way to larger achievements.

- Start with identifying specific aspects of non-verbal communication you find challenging.

- Break down these challenges into smaller, focussed objectives.

- Give yourself a realistic timeframe to work on each objective.

Celebrating Small Wins

Every step forward, no matter how minor it may seem, is a victory in the journey toward understanding others more deeply. Celebrate the moments of insight, the successful interpretations, and even the realization of mistakes—each is a valuable part of your growth. These celebrations reinforce positive progress and motivate you to continue your efforts.

- Keep a log of your successes and the new insights gained.

- Share your progress with friends or mentors who support your growth.

- Reward yourself for meeting your goals, reinforcing the value of your efforts.

Patience in Practice

Patience is your ally in the pursuit of mastering this complex skill. Accept that there will be times of frustration, confusion, and even setback. These moments are not indicators of failure but rather signs of the intricate nature of human behavior. With patience, you give yourself the grace to grow at your own pace, understanding that mastery is not an overnight achievement but the result of consistent, dedicated effort.

- Remind yourself that deep understanding comes from continuous observation and engagement.

- When you encounter challenges, take them as opportunities to learn rather than obstacles.

Long-Term Commitment

Committing to the long-term process of learning to read people is a testament to your dedication to personal and professional development. This commitment involves not just the active pursuit of knowledge but also a willingness to remain open to new perspectives and approaches. It's a dynamic process that evolves with each interaction, enriched by the diversity of human experiences and emotions you encounter.

- Recognize that this skill will develop and deepen over the entirety of your personal and professional life.

- Regularly seek out new resources, experiences, and perspectives to broaden your understanding.

- Engage with a community of learners who share your interest in human behavior, offering mutual support and insight.

In this journey, we've navigated the nuances of setting achievable goals, the importance of recognizing and celebrating each step forward, the crucial role of patience, and the commitment required to truly understand the depth of human interactions. These practices not only enhance our ability to read others but also enrich our connections, fostering a deeper empathy and appreciation for the complexity of the human experience.

As we close this chapter, we are reminded that the pursuit of understanding others is a continuous path of discovery. Each interaction offers a new perspective, each challenge a lesson, and each triumph a step closer to a richer, more nuanced understanding of the world around us. Moving forward, let us carry these insights as tools not only for personal growth but for building bridges of understanding and empathy in every aspect of our lives.

References

- *Micro Expressions | Facial Expressions* https://www.paulekman.com/resources/micro-expressions/

- *First impressions count* https://www.apa.org/gradpsych/2012/11/first-impressions

- *Inside the debate about power posing: a Q & A with Amy Cuddy* https://ideas.ted.com/inside-the-debate-about-power-posing-a-q-a-with-amy-cuddy/

- *You're Cramping My Style: Cultural Differences in ...* https://cultureplusconsulting.com/2015/06/15/cultural-differences-in-non-verbal-communication/

- *Improving Emotional Intelligence (EQ)* https://www.helpguide.org/articles/mental-health/emotional-intelligence-eq.htm

- *The Difference Between Empathy vs. Sympathy* https://www.betterup.com/blog/empathy-vs-sympathy

- *Experimental evidence of massive-scale emotional ...* https://www.pnas.org/doi/full/10.1073/pnas.1320040111

- *Six Emotional Leadership Styles - Mind Tools*
  https://www.mindtools.com/as8cal8/six-emotional-
  leadership-
  styles#:~:text=Therefore%20emotional%20intellige
  nce%20(EI)%20is,people%20who%20you're%20lea
  ding.

- *Maslow's Hierarchy of Needs*
  https://www.simplypsychology.org/maslow.html

- *Big Five Personality Traits: The 5-Factor Model of
  Personality* https://www.simplypsychology.org/big-
  five-personality.html

- *The Impact of Cognitive Biases on Professionals'
  Decision ...*
  https://www.ncbi.nlm.nih.gov/pmc/articles/PMC876
  3848/#:~:text=For%20instance%2C%20people%20t
  end%20to,and%20expectations%20(confirmation%2
  0bias).

- *Research on Non-verbal Signs of Lies and Deceit: A
  Blind ...*
  https://www.frontiersin.org/articles/10.3389/fpsyg.2
  020.613410

- *Communicating in the New Normal: Digital Body
  Language ...*
  https://www.aesc.org/insights/magazine/article/com
  municating-new-normal-digital-body-language-
  erica-dhawan

- *Pros & cons: impacts of social media on mental
  health*
  https://bmcpsychology.biomedcentral.com/articles/1
  0.1186/s40359-023-01243-x

- *Deception detection using ML and DL techniques* https://www.sciencedirect.com/science/article/pii/S2949719124000050

- *The Role of Empathy in Building a Thriving Social Media Community* https://www.kubbco.com/blog/the-role-of-empathy-in-building-a-thriving-social-media-community

- *Research on Non-verbal Signs of Lies and Deceit: A Blind Alley* https://www.ncbi.nlm.nih.gov/pmc/articles/PMC7767987/#:~:text=Psychological%20folklore%20tells%20us%20that,movements%2C%20frequent%20body%20posture%20changes.

- *HOW LEADERS CAN COMMUNICATE TO BUILD TRUST* https://iveybusinessjournal.com/publication/how-leaders-can-communicate-to-build-trust/

- *Ethics Code for Behavior Analysts | BACB* https://www.bacb.com/wp-content/uploads/2022/01/Ethics-Code-for-Behavior-Analysts-230119-a.pdf

- *Emotion and the Art of Negotiation* https://hbr.org/2015/12/emotion-and-the-art-of-negotiation

- *13 Emotional Intelligence Activities, Exercises & PDFs* https://positivepsychology.com/emotional-intelligence-exercises/

- *Behavioral Anomalies and Investigative Interviewing - LEB* https://leb.fbi.gov/articles/featured-articles/reading-people-behavioral-anomalies-and-investigative-interviewing

- *Ideas for Role-Play Scenarios for Social Skills Development* https://www.twinkl.com/blog/ideas-for-role-play-scenarios-for-social-skills-development

- *Seven Keys to Effective Feedback* https://www.ascd.org/el/articles/seven-keys-to-effective-feedback

- *How to Tell If Someone Is Lying to You, According to Experts* https://time.com/5443204/signs-lying-body-language-experts/

- *Understanding Biases And Their Impact On Our Perceptions* https://www.forbes.com/sites/forbescoachescouncil/2018/09/19/understanding-biases-and-their-impact-on-our-perceptions/

- *Active Listening: The key of successful communication in ...* https://www.ncbi.nlm.nih.gov/pmc/articles/PMC4844478/

- *Building your resilience - American Psychological Association* https://www.apa.org/topics/resilience/building-your-resilience

www.ingramcontent.com/pod-product-compliance
Lightning Source LLC
Chambersburg PA
CBHW051448130726
47987CB00005B/2232